Technique of Psychoanalytic Therapy

TECHNIQUE OF PSYCHOANALYTIC THERAPY

by

Sandor Lorand, M.D.

St. Martin's Press
New York

Copyright © 1982 by Sandor Lorand
For information, write: St. Martin's Press
175 Fifth Avenue, New York, N.Y. 10010
Manufactured in the United States of America

Library of Congress Cataloging in Publication Data

Lorand, Sándor, 1892-
    Technique of psychoanalytic therapy.

    Reprint. Originally published: New York :
International Universities Press, 1946.
    Bibliography: p.
    1. Psychoanalysis.   2.   Psychotherapy.
I.   Title.
RC504.L59   1982   616.89'17   81-21519
ISBN 0-312-78779-0   AACR2
ISBN 0-312-78780-9 (pbk.)

First published in the U.S.A. by International Universities Press, Inc.

CONTENTS

PREFACE TO THE SECOND EDITION

In these lectures there are a number of suggestions pertaining to the technique of handling patients in the therapeutic process. I have long been interested in the discussion of technique in a manner that would make it easier for the therapist to formulate his initial approach to treating his patient, and enable the patient himself to understand the problems which brought him to analysis. There is as much need for this discussion today as there was when these lectures first appeared in print in 1946.

So much of the technique of psychoanalysis involves the presentation of the patient's problems in terms of a central triad of feeling, thinking and acting. Once the patient understands that his problems originate within this framework he can be encouraged to talk about them in easy conversation with the therapist. The patient will then move toward a clearer recognition and acceptance of his problems and thus will find better ways to work through them.

I believe this triadic approach of feeling, thinking and acting is valid not only in solving technical problems of psychoanalytic therapy, but in understanding the sources of neurotic problems in general.

Sandor Lorand

Dec. 29, 1981
New York City

PREFACE

This volume is based on an advanced seminar and colloquium in technique which I have been giving at the New York Psychoanalytic Institute for the past four years, and also gave at the Philadelphia Psychoanalytic Institute for one semester. The course consists of a systematic discussion of technical procedures and of special technical problems. Requests of many of the physicians in training for mimeographed copies of the seminars have prompted my decision to put the material into book form.

It is not possible in a work of this type to cover all the problems pertaining to the technique of psychoanalysis. Moreover, occasional repetitions are inevitable since the material is a somewhat overlapping combination of technical papers, books on various developmental phases of psychoanalytic technique, my experience in clinical psychoanalysis and in the training of young colleagues, whose discussions in the colloquium of special therapeutic problems have been incorporated in these pages.

The basic principles of technique of psychoanalytic therapy as set forth by Freud, remain valid today. There has been a gradual expansion of theory and evolution of technique in the more than fifty years which have elapsed since Freud first formulated his discoveries. Many early associates of Freud and later contributors to psychoanalysis elaborated on some basic rules and modified others. New methods based on clinical findings were added to the ones already in use. All analysts make use directly or indirectly of these new technical approaches. From the abundance of literature on technique I have tried to extract the most valuable contributions for presentation in this book, which treats of the technical handling of problems every analyst meets in his clinical work. (No attempt will be made to survey the development of psychoanalytic technique.)

As is true of many of those who were in personal contact with Ferenczi, my main interest is in problems of therapy and technique. I am aware that this volume is colored by my personal approach and that therein may lie one of its defects. But those who have had some experience, however slight, in analytic work, will easily be able to follow the material because their experiences have been similar, I am sure, to the situations discussed in these pages. Some widely experienced analysts whose approach has been somewhat different, may not be in full agreement regarding the methods of technique which I consider important. However, if there is agreement as to the therapeutic aim, in other words, accord as to the degree of improvement which must be achieved before the patient is considered well, it is possible to arrive at the same point, through different avenues of approach.

Borderline neuroses and psychoses have not been included in this volume, since they are not part of the course.

I wish to express my appreciation to the editors of *The International Journal of Psychoanalysis, The Psychoanalytic Quarterly, The Psychoanalytic Review* and *Psychosomatic Medicine,* for their kind permission to quote from articles published in those journals.

SANDOR LORAND, M.D.

New York, December 1945

Chapter I

INTRODUCTION

The technique of psychoanalytic therapy cannot be learned from books and lectures alone. The method of learning is for the most part centered in the analysis of the future analyst. In that way only can he learn the technique of treating others. It is of primary importance that the beginning analyst know his own unconscious as thoroughly as possible for that knowledge will enable him to recognize the unconscious tendencies in his patients' productions. At the International Congress at Innsbruck in 1927, an opinion was voiced to the effect that the analyst should be better analyzed than his patient. There is much wisdom in that remark, flippant as it may sound. In treating patients we sometimes have to be satisfied with practical results which enable the patient to get along better than he did previous to treatment, even though the results are superficial. But in the analysis of the therapist, the situation is quite different. He must know his own character, his peculiarities and his shortcomings. It is a prerequisite for being able to deal effectively with the patient's transference and with the analyst's counter-transference.

Before the 1920's analysis was more of an intellectual process and the emotional content of the transference situation was not analyzed. With preconceived ideas in mind, based on theoretical knowledge, the unconscious was investigated with a view to uncovering what the analyst presupposed to be there. The principles of technique were applied, not as the need arose, or according to the personality and flexibility of the therapist, but in accordance with a basic rule to interpret the unconscious. The technique was at times a hit and miss proposition with little or no elasticity in the application of technical rules.

The many modifications which are now used extensively have been developed since 1918, the date of the Budapest Congress. Until that time analytical therapy was mostly concerned with the instincts and their vicissitudes. From then on, the interest began to center on the whole personality, and interpretations were made in relationship to the transference situation. Freud himself, in many instances considered the influence of the personality of the analyst, second to interpretation, the most powerful tool of therapy. Analysts today must recognize the importance of educational influences in analytic therapy in helping the patient make new adjustments and adaptations. Interpretation must be dynamic. This presupposes an attitude towards the patient on the part of the analyst.

The most important factor in an analyst's attitude to his patients is *objectivity* and this is acquired in his personal analysis and supervised clinical work. It is no exaggeration to say that success in curing patients largely depends upon one's ability to remain objective. It should not be surprising, therefore, if in these chapters there seem to be frequent references to this quality in the analyst, the lack or disturbance of which definitely interferes with the effective handling of the patient.

Before turning to practical problems, I should like to discuss, if only briefly, the causes of the failures and disappointments that beginners experience. The beginning analyst is likely to be easily discouraged, to feel, as it were, a let-down after a successful start, and then may become hesitant in his approach to the patient. My object is to give some insight into the causes of these disappointments, by pointing out technical errors in the approach to certain situations.

In clinical conferences with students I emphasize the importance of a correct approach to the patient from the earliest contact. The first step is perhaps the telephone conversation, when the patient calls for an interview. It is not an uncommon experience to have a patient call for an urgent appointment when the analyst has no free time or is tired, and for him to feel that since the patient waited that long he can wait a day or so longer. The appointment is made for the following day or later, and then to the analyst's annoyance the patient does not appear. Very rarely does the analyst think the patient was justified. Certainly it is not unethical to refuse to see a patient immediately; however, as a psychotherapist, who must be capable of empathy with the patient in his distress, it is important to see him even if only for a short time. A physician would not refuse aid if the demand seemed urgent, and when a patient suffers mental anguish the situation warrants just as great attention. Patients who come to us usually do so as a last resort. It is therefore extremely important to have a sympathetic approach from the first contact. The good will and sympathy of which the patient needs to be aware all through the treatment, must be felt in the initial contact.

Psychoanalytic treatment usually follows a general line and pattern. However, the guiding rules, about which so much is heard, i.e., free association, the reclining position, and so forth, cannot always be made use of exactly in accordance with the theoretical concept. After one or two years of supervised clinical work, one becomes aware of the necessity for variations and elasticity in the treatment of patients. An analyst may see, in succession, an anxious hysterical type of patient, then, an obsessive compulsive case, next a person with a character difficulty, then an impotent man in an aggressive mood, and finally a depressed patient. If the analyst is not sufficiently adaptable and relaxed, the different types of cases which follow one another cause a great strain, and it is possible and even likely that he will transfer the mood created by one patient to another.

It is natural for each of us to have his own technical approaches which are learned or acquired through having handled a variety of cases. After four or five years of work each analyst has developed his own approach and knows when to be cautious and when tolerant, when to be active and when passive. The therapist's over-sensitivity to the patients' reactions diminishes and his own reactions to the patients' positive feelings provoke less anxiety in him and prove less wearing.

In certain types of cases the therapeutic results definitely depend upon the personality of the analyst and his ability to adapt himself to the situations created by the patient. There are many excellent technical papers in the vast body of analytical literature which deal with that situation, showing through clinical material, how the analyst's adaptability and elasticity help make the patient accessible for therapy. On what does the accessibility of the patient depend? We know that the primary aim of the neurotic individual is to avoid pain and frustration. Therapy endeavors to break down the established patterns of behavior and enable the patient to tolerate the inevitable pains and frustrations of life. This is a process the patient will, of course, resist. In his resistance he uses various kinds of defense mechanisms such as repression, reaction formation, inhibition, projection, displacement, intellectualization, reality denial, sublimation, etc. The therapeutic process must constantly utilize various technical means to combat these defenses.

The analyst's attitude, to which, as was pointed out earlier, the patient is sensitive from the first moment of contact, plays a definite role in the therapy. The patient's resistance, which arises automatically, can be weakened or strengthened by this attitude, from the very beginning. The attitude must be one of tolerance and benevolence, and the best way to hold on to it in trying moments is to think of the patient as a helpless, weak, inhibited child (which indeed he is) who will have to reach emotional maturity under the analyst's guidance, mainly through the transference relationship.

The core of every neurosis is anxiety, which has its roots in the person's early childhood. Together with aggression and guilt, which are always bound up with anxiety, it moulds the behavior pattern from early childhood through adolescence, finally bringing about the neurotic conflicts and symptoms from which the individual is driven to seek relief.

At the onset of treatment, the patient must feel a certain amount of security in order to comply with the first important requirement in analysis: free association. Those who have had experience with different attitudes of patients at the start of their analysis, know that the varying reactions depend upon the type of neurosis from which the patient suffers. Intuitive understanding is required in order to appreciate fine nuances of emotional need of individual patients. One must practise the *art* of analysis, based on clinical experience. In his own analysis, the therapist frees himself of anxiety and learns to relax, with the result that he is able to handle his cases objectively.

In clinical seminars, from time to time young colleagues have raised questions pertaining to the rules for analytic procedure, the strict observance of which is considered by some analysts to be essential. For instance, these students had already met with patients who refused to recline on the couch and they (the students) were uncertain of what their attitude should be. Patients with acute anxiety often want to sit up facing the analyst, and may maintain that attiude for a period. In such cases the analyst's first objective should be to reduce the anxiety. To insist that the patient recline and to state that analysis cannot proceed in any other way, is a mistake. There are many reasons for the patient's desire to sit up and in the course of analysis there will be ample opportunity to discover them. The most obvious, of course, is that patients want the reassurance of observing the analyst's attitude by evaluating his facial expressions. They also want to maintain the direct contact, which would preclude probing deeper into unconscious motivations. There may be other unconscious reasons as well; all are connected with the patient's many fears.

One patient sat opposite me for fifteen analytic hours before she was ready to take the reclining position. She was a young married woman, whose various anxieties inhibited her going out into the street or to the theatre, while at the same time she feared being home alone. She was afraid that she would become dizzy and collapse. Behind this fear lay conscious anxieties concerning a heart attack. After the first few visits she felt somewhat reassured, took up her household duties and even resumed a fairly active social life, which she had been slowly giving up. But soon the discussion of daily routines, her attitude toward children, family· relationships and her fears in connection with all three, came to an end and she felt that there was nothing more for her to talk about.

I brought to her attention the possibility of her having fantasies and day-dreams. At first she was reluctant to recognize their existence and countered by subjecting me to a period of questioning (as many patients do at the start of analysis). Would analysis harm her? What could she expect from the treatment? Did she really need analysis? And then, did all women have day-dreams?

It was a method of seeking reassurance and one may perhaps doubt the wisdom of giving it, since it has been stated that analysis must proceed in an atmosphere in which the patient experiences frustration. Experience proves, however, that the guidance and support which the analyst gives does not in any way fulfill the patient's need for love. To be sure, when the analyst gives encouragement, he must always analyze and interpret with the patient his anxiety and need for encouragement. If that procedure is followed, the anxiety and demand for reassurance gradually diminish. But the patient still experiences frustration because the demand for guidance and affection is so much greater than what the analyst can give.

The questions of this particular patient constituted an attempt to reassure herself that she was no different from other women in having day-dreams. Then her questions touched on the possibility of a happily married person having romantic fantasies. She was reassured that it was possible but she still continued to sit opposite me, because, as she said, she wanted to maintain her newly acquired feeling of well-being and relaxation. In addition, she stated that she could control herself better that way; she feared that lying down and relaxing control would permit thoughts to arise that would upset her. She volunteered the information that before each analytical hour, she prepared what she was going to say, because, when finding herself in the atmosphere of the analytic situation (about which she had read) she was reminded of a time before her marriage when she used to visit a man with whom she thought she was in love and she feared the association of thoughts might revive old romantic feelings.

One may argue, and perhaps with some justification, that if I had insisted from the start, on her reclining on the couch she would have brought out this material sooner because she would have relaxed her conscious control. That may be true, but years of experience have convinced me that it is unwise to insist, in the opening phase of analysis, on rules and strict procedure with any patient, certainly not with one who suffers from acute anxiety. It is important that the analyst not be rigid in such matters. To affirm, for instance, as some physicians do, that analysis can only proceed on a five hour a week basis, is also unwise. I have successfully analyzed patients who were only able to come three times a week and at the moment have a patient who comes twice a week from out of town. Of course his progress is slower than it would be if he were able to come more often, but he is having a real analysis nonetheless. Other analysts, I am sure, have done the same.

In the case of the woman who insisted upon sitting opposite me for so many hours, the analytical situation had to appear to offer, at least in the beginning, a more pleasant environment than her own home where actual difficulties surrounded her, and her parents' home where the troubles originated. The realization that she was not being censured by the analyst (at home she had been the butt of constant criticism) encouraged her to the extent that she began to speak without fear and to start on the road, through free associations, to the source of her deeper problems.

The wish to sit up and face me was obviously an expression of resistance. Her mode of speech, her somewhat flirtatious behavior, gave evidence of an incipient positive transference, which she feared while at the same time wishing to retain it. She herself gave as the reason for maintaining the sitting posture, her desire to hold on to pleasant feelings. This type of resistance is frequently found in the initial stage of analysis when positive feelings are used as a defense. In other types of cases, outstandingly negative attitudes are used for the same purpose. In her case the resistance was quite obviously directed against permitting unconscious drives to become conscious. At this early stage of analysis there already were indications that those unconscious impulses which she tried to keep in check by preparing in advance the subject matter of her interview and refusing to lie down, were of a sexual nature. Moreover, she felt secure in the emotional relationship and was unwilling to disturb it. Her pattern of experience in the past, especially in early childhood, having demonstrated that affection and attachment end in frustration and discomfort, she was now at all pains to avoid a repetition of the early disappointments.

It is important for the therapist to be aware not only of the conscious defenses, but also of the various types of resistance which originate in the different parts of the personality and impede the progress of therapy. They may, for the most part, be unconscious and the analyst must be on the alert for their manifestations, which have to be analyzed and interpreted whenever they arise.

The nature and character of defenses are determined by their source. A drive that was powerfully rejected because of its anti-social nature will exert strong defenses against emerging into consciousness, thus creating a potent resistance to its analysis. An impulse which was repressed at a very early age because of fear and guilt will also create a strong resistance when analysis endangers its insulation. The continuous task of therapy is to make unconscious impulses conscious and to make the repressed material accessible to the patient, all of which is accomplished through combatting and eliminating resistances. The patient must be made aware of the fact that he uses all manner of resistance against change even though that is the very purpose for which he has come to analysis.

At the same time, one should not forget the role of the conscious desires and actual experiences in the creation and maintenance of defense mechanisms, as well as the influence of the repressed material. The appreciation of reality and conscious factors was always emphasized by Freud and his school.

It is not uncommon for a beginning analyst to find that after a period of good work and apparent progress, sometimes lasting for months, the patient brings up the same problems which were discussed and seemingly eliminated. For example, a patient with strong voyeuristic tendencies, seemed after a few months to have lost them, and became more courageous and aggressive in his work and social relations. Suddenly his old behavior pattern reappeared and his dreams once more gave evidence of strong castration fears and escape tendencies. The analyst complained, during a supervised hour, that the patient was not making any progress, that his productions were all repetitious; he stated that the patient knew all the ramifications of his problem but was not doing anything about them. Obviously, the analyst was discouraged.

The return of the behavior pattern was nothing more than a new wave of resistance provoked by his conscious preoccupation with changing to a better job, thus making himself more independent. The conscious endeavor threatened his old pattern of behavior which had sheltered him from all the dangers that growing up, independence, and sexual maturity meant to him. The attempt to change, feeble though it was, aroused renewed resistance and caused the reappearance of past behavior patterns and regressive trends. Progress meant facing competition. Such situations were charged with the emotional involvements belonging to the Oedipus period: the aggression towards parents which existed side by side with the wish for dependence and love. To secure the latter, he believed that he had to remain at a childhood level, especially in his sexual behavior. The recurrence of symptoms and types of behavior is typical of the early phase of analysis, when the roots of the neurotic symptoms and behavior patterns begin to be uncovered. As a result of the transference relationship, the patient's reaction to the analysis will gradually show a correlation with his childhood reactions and attitudes. From that point on, the analyst's attention must be focussed on interpretation of the patient's behavior and productions in relation to current reality situations, childhood and developmental periods and to the analytical situation.

When the patient recognizes the origin, meaning and aim of his neurotic conflicts and symptoms, he makes a conscious effort to change. However, the anxiety provoked by new undertakings and responsibilities, partially under the impact of reality, but mainly resulting from unconscious fear and guilt, will induce him to try to maintain the old familiar mode of reaction. Resistances will constantly be in operation against the conscious attempts at changing. From the unconscious will come forth a warning refrain: "Don't change, don't change." In the patient's dreams especially, the fear of change and warning against it will be found. In cases of sexual difficulties, at the point where the patient begins to modify his or her attitude ever so slightly, the fears concerning sexuality having decreased, and he or she reaches out to attempt a step in the direction of heterosexuality, there will always be some expression in the dream of a contradiction of the conscious effort, as though a voice from the deep unconscious were warning: "It is dangerous to become involved with the opposite sex." One must have infinite patience and be tireless in interpreting and re-interpreting dreams and behavior, in order to overcome this constantly recurring resistance. The patient may be hostile to the analyst's interpretations because of his own dawning realization of the meaning of his behavior, and some slight insight into its causes. Recognizing that the interpretation is a push forward, he automatically will resist. Such reactions serve to ventilate hostility which the patient has been afraid to express in the past. After repeated interpretations the patient develops an understanding of his problems and gradually realizes that his attitude to the analyst is a reactivation of early childhood attitudes to parental authority, against which, because of fear and guilt, he was unable to express the hostility he felt, and that he is now re-experiencing it as a delayed reaction.

In the transference relationship, every attitude has to be completely interpreted in this manner. The same holds true for erotic and tender feelings expressed in connection with the analyst. The present must always be connected with the past so that the patient understands that his emotional reactions are really "transferred" from another developmental period to the present.

Through superficial interpretations in the beginning of analysis, the patient learns to evaluate his symptoms and illness differently. As he progresses to a greater acceptance of his fantasies and emotions, we must be aware of the difficulties in store for him. An hysterical type of patient may start with strong transference feelings and progress rapidly, but when deeply repressed material is reached, he becomes blocked and anxious. The obsessional type, on the other hand, may be thoroughly negative from the start. Both need delicate handling and an acute awareness on the part of the analyst, of the struggle which lies ahead.

Chapter II

INTERPRETATION

The central problem of technique is the management of the transference, since the corrective process is accomplished through that relationship. Therefore the emotional implications, including the resistances in connection with the transference relationship, are of cardinal importance in analysis. As one proceeds with treatment, it becomes obvious that the therapy automatically divides into different phases (to which Ferenczi drew attention early in the development of technique). The first phase is taken up with concentrating on the patient's life history given with free associations, getting a picture of his behavior patterns and the history of their development, especially through observation of the nature of the patient's transference manifestations. In this phase the analyst's job is to observe and to encourage the patient to express his thoughts and feelings. With the realization that he is not being criticised, the patient loses some of his fear and guilt, hence the spontaneous improvement in the first phase. It is necessary to give some superficial interpretation at times, but as nearly as possible the transference should be left out of the discussion.

The second phase is marked by slow development of resistance in the patient as he becomes aware of his problems and realizes that he himself must do something about them. The transference relationship becomes prominent and its continual interpretation is of the greatest importance. The analyst becomes the center of the patient's desires for love, guidance, help, and the solution of all his problems. The desires not being realized, he then becomes the focal point of the patient's aggression. When that happens, resistance moves into the foreground. Reviewing the patient's behavior, connecting his current attitudes with his attitudes to people in the past, especially to those persons whom the analyst replaces in the patient's thoughts and fantasies, must be done over and over again.

This phase leads gradually to a weakening of the transference (the third phase) and the patient slowly learns to do things by himself, to be self-reliant. From time to time there will be a revival of the old desires for dependence on the analyst, which will result in repeated feelings of frustration, leading the patient to again try to stand on his own feet. The ego of the patient becomes gradually stronger until he is actually able to give up his dependence upon the analyst.

Breaking down resistance and alleviating anxiety are continual tasks during the second and third phases. The analyst must understand, and at times sense intuitively the patient's need to put the therapist into different roles in accordance with his unconscious desires and feelings.

The process can be summarized briefly as follows: the patient re-lives his past in the transference relationship, but this time under favorable circumstances for emotional reactions. Interpretation of his varying attitudes towards the analyst clarifies his problems and helps him understand his projections, unconscious fears and repressed desires. It is of course important that the analyst not act the role assigned to him by the patient (for instance, accepting the father or mother role and giving an exaggerated degree of approval, help, or disapproval), because by so doing he makes the transference situation a reality, fixing the analysis at that point and preventing further progress.

There is no definite rule as to when interpretation should begin. Young colleagues have occasionally shown insecurity about timing the start of interpretation. This hesitancy was caused by their having been supervised by more than one teacher, no two of whom agreed upon exactly the same starting point.

There are also differences of opinion regarding other aspects of interpretation, for instance, whether it should be elaborate or concise. Whatever approach is used, the results can be good. The important thing is for the analyst to *know what he is doing and why.* That ability can only be acquired through experience.

When to begin interpretation depends a great deal on the type of case. The deciding factor is the patient's need. Early interpretation is indicated in anxiety cases, in order to reassure the patient. I have found it necessary in many of these cases to interpret right from the start, but in so doing to adhere strictly to the disturbing symptoms and the material that has been produced, interpreting only as much as the patient can digest. However, in other cases one can be conservative and wait for more material. Timing also depends upon the elasticity of the analyst. That quality inclines him to *active* participation at certain stages of analysis.

When analysis has progressed sufficiently and the patient produces material concerning oral, anal, and genital conflicts, I consider it essential before interpreting to give the patient a brief sketch of the physiological and psychological developments of these zones, and to explain, for instance, that food intake (sucking) carries pleasure sensations which are retained in adult life and given expression in smoking, gum chewing, and the like; also, that the physiological function of the anus produces pleasure sensations. Then the ground is prepared for an explanation of the child's use of anal functioning to express compliance and love or defiance and hate (anal sadism) in relationship to parents. In connection with the genital phase of development, it is necessary to point out that urination and sensations in the genital region are sources of pleasure for the child. These sensations can be of a masturbatory quality. Since preoccupation with the genitals is prohibited by parents, fear and guilt accompany indulgence in genital play; parental interference creates aggression; thus the child can also express compliance or defiance through touching or refraining from touching his genitals.

The linking up of the physiological with the psychological makes it easier for the patient to comprehend that these phenomena have been at work within him, contributing to his symptomatology.

I emphasize this type of elaboration in early interpretation (as an example of more active participation) because my experience in supervising beginning analysts has shown that they often neglect to interpret in detail the influence of the developmental phases on adult life. Thus, when treatment is advanced and they use the terms "oral, anal, and genital fixation" in interpreting the behavior of patients, they have little effect. For instance, the term "anal sadism" is frequently used to describe the patient's aggressive behavior, but the analyst often has difficulty in explaining the origin of the anal sadism.

Sometimes in the early phase of analysis, a dream gives the analyst the opportunity to elaborate on the problem of early development and provides a convenient introduction for the patient to his deeply rooted problems. One of my patients, a borderline case, was in the habit of getting up several times during the night to urinate. He attributed it to weakness of the bladder and other physical causes. It was apparent very early in his treatment however, that the frequency of urination served as a masturbation equivalent and was connected with repressed sexual stimuli. (He was in his early thirties, had strong, repressed homo-sexual tendencies but no sexual experience.) He dreamed the following: "A girl comes towards me and embraces me." He awoke to find that he had urinated. He changed to dry garments, went back to sleep and dreamed: "I saw a number of men and they looked menacing to me."

The second part of the dream was not discussed at that time because of its paranoid and homosexual implications. However, the first part provided the opportunity of discussing the whole genital phase of development, as was briefly outlined above, and he was able to see that urine and semen were identical to his unconscious, also that at the present stage he could only permit himself to use his penis for the same function for which he had used it in childhood: urination. That led us easily and naturally into a discussion of all his fears concerning women, sex, and so forth.

Too often one hears young analysts say: "The patient is now working through the anal phase of his analysis" or the "oral phase", whatever he considers the case to be. There is no such isolated section in any personality development. The oral and anal phases overlap; both fuse with the genital and the interaction of all three forms an important part of the structure of the personality. It is a different matter when analysts isolate the three phases in order to facilitate the discussion of theory among themselves; but when dealing with dynamic concepts and with the emotions of the patient, the total personality and its reactions must be worked with as a unit.

It is my conviction, shared, I am sure, by many analysts, that the method of interpreting in terms of particular developmental levels meets with little success and tends to intellectualize analysis instead of achieving a working-through of emotional experience which brings about real understanding.

Questions arise as to whether one should interpret in every analytic session, and as to when, during the session, to offer interpretation. These points must be left to the analyst's judgment. Ferenczi's opinion was that one should never let a patient leave the office in great distress or suspense. "Try to interpret and alleviate his pain, as the surgeon, before the patient leaves, makes him feel better by putting a nice fresh bandage on the wound." A number of analysts of my acquaintance leave interpretation for the end of the hour. One of my colleagues described that as giving the patient a little bundle to take along with him when he leaves, so that he has something to think about until his return.

One must be able to judge whether the patient's productions are important enough to warrant interpretation and how much elaboration the patient needs in order to understand his conflicts and be able to proceed. One rule is of decisive importance: interpret when you observe resistance developing in the patient.

A practical example is the case of a young man who was in treatment for sexual impotence. His general neurotic symptoms were negligible and caused him little difficulty, but he was getting on in years and began to realize that being unadjusted sexually was an important problem. He made rapid progress in analysis, developed a strong transference to his female analyst and brought forth a wealth of sexual material. One day when he was alone he found himself thinking of his analyst and wanting to be in her house with her. Until that time his transference manifestations had not been interpreted and when he suddenly realized that he was thinking of his analyst he became frightened. During the next analytical session he was very much embarrassed and his productions ceased. When urged to express his thoughts and feelings, he brought forth the fantasy of being with her, and in relating it expressed resentment against her for encouraging sexual fantasies and dreams, the discussion of which prompted him to bring still more material, all of which served to upset and confuse him.

In this case the analyst was a trifle insecure and therefore had avoided interpretation and discussion of the transference. The result was that the patient's sexual feelings provoked anxiety which had originated in early childhood in connection with sexual activities. Lack of timely interpretation brought about the patient's negative attitude.

The patient's conscious attitude (ego) must also be in the foreground of the analyst's attention. Bearing it in mind, he can make comprehensible and conscious to the patient the way in which his repressed feelings and impulses influence his conscious attitude in analysis. The patient gradually comes to realize, through repeated interpretations, that repressions in his adult life are maintained by the guilt and fear carried over from early childhood rebellion; further, that these childhood feelings were repressed, the result being that the actual conscious reactions of adulthood are bound up with the unconscious affects and influenced by them.

In our persistent interpretation of the unconscious, we must take into consideration, in addition to the influence of the repressed unconscious past, the patient's ego reactions. Only in this way can a change be effected in the conscious attitude of the patient, and a healthier relationship established between the ego, superego, and id. That implies making the ego stronger and therefore less afraid of the superego with its threats of punishment, at the same time making the superego more tolerant of the emerging id impulses.

The time most favorable to start interpretation is when there is sufficient evidence of the presence of the transference and enough material produced by the patient to convince him of the validity of the interpretations. Different types of neuroses react differently to interpretation. The reactions of the above-

cited case of sexual difficulty indicate that early interpretation of transference is of advantage in such cases.
It stimulates the patient to produce material relating
to the unconscious because the interpretation has
given him some understanding of the source of his
feelings about the analyst and he is somewhat relieved
of embarrassment and discomfort by the reassurance
that the feelings really belong to childhood and have
been "transferred."

While on the subject of reassurance, I want to
emphasize the fact that it should not be confused with
interpretation. The patient must be aware that when
he is reassured it is for the immediate therapeutic
purpose, but he should nonetheless feel that the analyst's words are sincere attempts to ease his discomfort.
He should also be made to realize that reassurance
is not the main therapeutic tool of psychoanalysis, but
a temporary adjuvant. The analyst himself should
avoid making it a habit and should be alert for the
occasions when the patient is in actual need of reassurance. When the patient is negativistic, reassurance not
only has no value, but may even have the opposite
effect, i.e., make the patient feel that the analyst is over-
anxious and helpless. The same holds true when the
analyst introduces himself as an example to reassure
the patient. As to *how* to reassure: one has to feel
one's way, and here again, only through experience
does one learn the various methods of putting the
patient at ease.

In the beginning stage of analysis, an anxious, hysterical patient may cry and plead for help. An understanding of the sources of an attack of panic makes it
easier to alleviate such anxiety. The analyst's atti-

tude to the patient, his behavior during these sessions, even his manner of speaking, can all help in reassuring the patient.

The start of analysis may present many difficulties to the patient and in certain situations the analyst must, by means of reassurance, help the patient overcome initial obstacles. If a patient begins his hour in silence the analyst must understand the meaning of it or at least have some idea of what it refers to, and help the patient to start to speak. If such a situation is not handled correctly the solution of the patient's problem concerning the silence becomes more and more difficult. A patient who for a while had tried analysis with another colleague, and had spent weeks reclining on the couch in silence, was not able to speak to me at first either. She began to talk after being encouraged to write down what was on her mind. What she wrote was a series of genital and anal obscenities and it became evident immediately that she could not speak for fear those expressions would slip through the conscious guard and appear in her speech. (The former analyst had insisted on her speaking, although she herself had wanted to write down her thoughts.)

If patients struggle with silence, I try to interpret it for them and in a simple way convey its emotional implications. I bring to their attention the fact that of their own volition they have come for treatment, that the means of being cured is through voicing their thoughts and feelings; by coming they have carried out in part their desire to be treated, but through silence they block the progress of the cure, in fact render it impossible. I suggest that perhaps they are afraid of my disapproval, or their pride does not permit them to relate some incident. If still unsuccessful I offer them the possible interpretation that their silence is caused by something about me personally. Perhaps they may not have liked some interpretation given in the previous interview, or the manner in which it was said; possibly they have had some thoughts about me before coming to the hour, some fantasy or dream which they do not want to divulge. Usually one of these suggestions induces the patient to talk.

A colleague whom I supervised, had a difficult time with a male patient, who for a long period would not talk and at times even fell asleep during the analytical session. It turned out that he was repeating a habit pattern of many years standing. He felt compelled to take a nap at a certain hour of the afternoon, even if only for twenty minutes. Before starting analysis, no matter where he was, he rushed home, undressed and went to sleep. The days he fell asleep at the analyst's office proved to be the days when his analytical hour coincided with his napping time. The habit was developed unconsciously, as a means of breaking up the daily routine, with which he found it difficult to cope. His sleeping during the analytical hour was an expression of his strong defense against changing and fear that his defenses would be broken. All interpretations and other attempts of the analyst to keep him awake were in vain. I suggested jolting the couch and it proved effective. The patient became very much irritated and that feeling led to a disclosure of his original defensive habit of going to sleep at a certain hour of the day to escape the irritations of reality.

Silence or difficulty in expressing thoughts are typical defense reactions. The patient is usually unaware
of the conflict that he is trying to avoid by not talking
and may also be unaware of his defense. Uncovering
the defense results in weakened resistance. Feeling
reassured of the analyst's understanding, the patient
brings forth more deeply repressed material. Silence,
as well as other mechanisms of defense, must be carefully and thoroughly dissected, so that the repressed
drives can be made conscious and acceptable.

The silence defense is frequently bound up with
feelings pertaining to current situations in analysis.
One of my patients spent part of an analytical session
in stubborn refusal to talk. It proved to be her
defense against discussing a plan of seeing a male
friend with whom she had indulged in sexual play.
On those occasions, the relationship was to all appear-
ances analyzed, interpreted, and worked through. At
the time that the silence occurred, however, her attitude to me was one of spite and defiance and her plan
to consummate the sexual relationship was a direct
result of her aggressive attitude towards me. She
was afraid to talk about her plans, knowing that discussing them might cause her to change her mind.
She thus used the silence as a defense against my
interference with the realization of her projected
sexual activity.

A defense against expressing drives and impulses
may become the resistance, as, for instance, in the case
of a patient who gets off at the wrong floor in order
to avoid coming to the analytical session where she
will have to report direct sexual fantasies about the
analyst. Defenses sometimes vary with different types

of neuroses. A great variety of defense mechanisms are to be found in character neuroses. Outstanding among them is the faculty of covering up one emotion with the display of another, sometimes the opposite; for instance, permanent smiling when there is present a deep, underlying sadness, or, hypomania to hide depression. It is not uncommon for such patients to be cynical and ironic instead of showing open aggression, or to be self-critical because they fear criticism. Another type of defense is playfulness, by means of which the patient tries to control the process of analysis. Some patients try to provoke arguments with a view to putting the analyst on the defensive. Others intellectualize because of fear of displaying feeling. All these defenses work together in character neuroses to create the well known rigidity which is such a barrier to analytical progress.

In hysterical patients a characteristic defense is repression of the past—not being able to remember what has happened. This type of patient turns sadistic tendencies into masochistic ones, suffering instead of inflicting pain, being fearful instead of aggressive.

In compulsion neuroses, the outstanding defense is isolation: the patient is completely unaware of the object of his symptom. His anxiety is disconnected from the content of the threat. One of my patients is an instructive example of that type. He is constantly preoccupied with making certain that the gas jets are closed when he goes to bed, gets up to investigate many times during the night and has not the slightest idea of what compels him to that repetitious action which is such a torture to him. Analysis reveals many meanings in the obsessional symptom. Outstanding

among them are: obedience to an unconscious superego command to carry out a task, and expiation, making good a repressed, unconscious hostile drive.
Another characteristic defense mechanism in compulsion neurosis is negation, the object of which is to
allay all possible conflicts resulting from antagonistic
strivings within the patient. The best example of
negation is the obsessional prayer, which is a frantic
attempt to suppress the rising tide of rebellion against
superego——God.

In order to recognize and handle different types of
defense reactions, analysts must have a basic understanding of the sources of the defenses and an appreciation of the patient's difficulties in facing his problems.
The examples cited above give some indication of the
sources. One must be versatile and continually analyze the *resistance,* which is always a reaction of the
ego to the emergence of impulses from the unconscious. The object of therapy is to bring forth into
consciousness the very same drives against which the
resistance is directed. The task becomes more difficult in cases where the defenses against experiencing
pain and frustration have become an established pattern. All neurotic individuals make much greater
attempts to avoid pain and frustration than do normal
people. Therapy points in the opposite direction, its
object being to enable the patient to tolerate frustration. It is only to be expected, therefore, that the
patient will *resist* the therapy. Analysts must also bear
in mind the fact that most defenses arise automatically
during the process of analysis, and in order for the
patient to be able to counteract them, he needs to be
made fully aware of their origin, object, and function.

Beginners often ask for rules. What is the best way to handle the patient's defenses and resistances? What is the best attitude for the analyst to assume in order not to increase, but rather reduce, the resistances? As to the analyst's attitude toward his patient, Glover expressed it by saying that *the ideal is absence of dogmatic attitude.* Freud's original suggestion that analysis should be carried out in a state of abstinence, meaning that the patient should learn to tolerate frustration in analysis and that the analyst's attitude should maintain that frustrating atmosphere (passivity), is given varying interpretations. Freud did not mean that the patient should have no satisfaction during analysis. He related abstinence to symptom gratification. In all types of neuroses patients find various kinds of substitute gratification, all of which the analyst will have to dam up in order to eliminate the main symptom. This process naturally provokes hostility and resistance. All kinds of new symptoms will be created to divert the analyst's efforts or to prove that the patient does not need analysis. Various symptoms, somatic in appearance, set in, thus forcing the analyst to secure the opinion of an internist.

One of my patients who was well advanced in analysis (it seemed that the completion was only a few months off, and it turned out to be so) had a dream that indicated she was hiding something from me. I mentioned that possibility to her, not insisting that she disclose what it was, but telling her to think about what there could possibly be that she did not want to discuss with me. It was a short transference dream and at the time it occurred the patient was seriously contemplating marriage. To bring her to that point had taken over three years of analysis. Prior to treatment her psycho-sexual development had never progressed farther than puberty level. She still had some difficulty, however, in accepting the ideas of actual consummation of the sexual act, pregnancy, and permanent attachment to one man.

In the very next analytical session she admitted that she had consciously avoided mentioning the fact that she had vaginal pains on that particular day. She was aware of the meaning of the pains and knew that a discussion would inevitably lead to an admission of very intimate petting with her fiancé, involving external genital contact which produced very pleasurable sensations. The extreme petting had created doubt in her mind as to whether she was still a virgin. The real object of the doubt was to be reassured not only verbally, but by physical examination and her embarrassment over the wish-fantasy of being examined by me, kept her from bringing up the entire matter.

Strict adherence to the fundamental rule would have meant insisting that the patient tell everything that was in her mind as soon as I suspected something was being withheld. Needless to say, this rule cannot be followed at all times.

Previous to that episode, the same patient succeeded in being preoccupied for a while with the symptom of shortness of breath, which she insisted was due to a cold and went to her family doctor for verification; but he could find nothing wrong. The symptom proved to be connected with her petting and masturbatory fantasies, which at that time she tried to avoid discussing. It was plain that the object of the symptom was to confuse the analyst and create difficulties in treatment.

At times there are contra-indications to active interference, as the following incident illustrates: to stop his patient's promiscuity, a young colleague threatened that the patient's analysis would be endless if she continued her sexual escapades. He said this during an analytical session when the patient was discussing her plans and the anticipated happenings of the following day's sexual encounter, dwelling in detail on her partner's sexual ability. Despite the analyst's threat, the patient kept her rendezvous, but did not come back to the analyst's office for the following few days. At my suggestion he telephoned her and induced her to resume treatment. When I discussed this doctor's attitude with him, it became evident that his counter-transference was involved. He was annoyed with the patient and not fully aware that his attitude to her sexual behavior was very nearly a replica of her own superego. After she returned to analysis, a discussion of her behavior and the analyst's threat brought to her mind her father's admonitions in childhood and adolescence when she was quite coquettish with boys and rather exhibitionistic. She stated that she believed her father's scoldings to have been unjust. The analyst had failed to see the challenge involved. Thus, instead of fully interpreting and working through her promiscuous tendencies, showing her that they were connected with her early rebellion against her father, he stepped in when the patient was unprepared to accept a suggestion, much less a prohibition.

Every suggestion to the patient creates a certain amount of conflict and may provoke unconscious resistance, while at the same time it strengthens the transference to the analyst. Active interference may also serve to gratify the masochistic tendencies of some patients. The analyst must be fairly certain of the patient's probable reactions before giving suggestions. Constant interpretation plus the analyst's technical ability can take care of all situations which arise in the course of treatment. The above-cited case is an example of how a bad situation can be corrected if the analyst is willing and able to alter his attitude and approach. Here the progress of analysis was resumed through the analyst's reviewing the whole situation with the patient and admitting to her that he had come to certain rather hasty conclusions, on the basis of which he had acted when attempting to interfere with her sexual activities.

As has been said many times, the analyst's attitude should not be rigid, nor should he always maintain a frustrating attitude towards the patient. At times benevolence must replace frustration. How much to allow one's self to express is a question every physician must decide for himself. Moreover, it will be found that one's attitude varies with each patient. To make an issue of passivity on the part of the analyst, is out-dated. One analyst can be either more dynamic than another or less, more detached or less, but the earlier demand that analysts be completely detached can hardly be followed. However, beginners are at times

active to a degree that restricts in an undesirable manner their patients' functioning.   In such cases the
analyst's activity adds to their neurotic inhibitions.
For instance, one colleague forbade his patient, after
eight months of analysis, to buy a new home.   He had
interfered with that plan of hers once before, at the
start of her treatment.   In his supervised training
period, he gave as the reason for his prohibition, that
the patient would have been completely involved in
plans for the house and would not have paid any
attention to her other problems.   In other words, he
felt that in buying a house she would be running away
from her problems.   (Incidentally, her husband
wanted the house and would have taken care of all
the details.)   There must of course be a middle road
between the extremes of passivity and activity.   The
beginner will be wise to be cautious until he learns
through experience how far to practise each.   There
is never complete passivity or complete detachment in
any analysis, because even passivity is conceived of by
the patient as the analyst's attitude to him and it is
reacted to as an active measure.

Freud himself used active measures in certain situations.   I refer to his suggestion to agoraphobic patients
to go out and face situations which create fears, in
order to mobilize the anxiety that is otherwise hidden
by defenses.   The modes of technical approach to
states of panic and anxiety have been briefly mentioned earlier in this volume; reference was made to
their immediate amelioration.   Though opinions differ
concerning the details of technical procedure, the
immediate object of therapy must be that of making

the patient aware of himself and his problems, of feelings which are covered up and which interfere with his happiness. The analyst must be capable of intense empathy with the patients' emotions, which, in anxieties and phobias, are near the surface and readily observable.

Chapter III

ANXIETIES AND PHOBIAS

The nucleus of anxieties and phobias is known to be the Oedipus problem and its vicissitudes. All the symptoms are connected with repressed sexual drives and they represent a compromise between the repressed erotic wishes and the repressive forces. Through the phobias, instinctual drives are displaced into the outer world, and thus an external situation becomes the object of fear. The symptoms aim at averting the danger of castration which threatens because of the genital drives involved. To illustrate the therapeutic proceedings, I shall present two abbreviated cases: one a severe anxiety hysteria and the other a horse phobia combined with a diffuse anxiety. Both were analyzed about fifteen years ago and have been very well adjusted since. They represent the type of neuroses, the psychopathology and symptomatology of which served as the experiment ground for Freud's investigations which led to the theoretical formulations of his basic psychoanalytic principles: his studies of hysterias which resulted in the discovery of the psychoanalytic method and technique of therapy.

The patient suffering from a severe anxiety hysteria [1] was a man in his thirties, who enjoyed a privileged economic and social status; but the city streets on which he walked, the house he lived in, the meadows and forests bordering his golf course, and

[1] "Fairy Tales and Neurosis", by S. Lorand. *Psychoanalytic Quarterly*, Vol. IV, 1935.

the lakes where he went fishing, were all filled with giants, ogres, witches, and strange animals. In his daily life he met friends whose faces at times appeared bird-like and whose noses seemed to protrude like beaks. In his dreams, strange prehistoric animals reached through the window; big and baby elephants, snakes, the wolf of *Little Red Riding Hood* appeared and gave rise to preoccupation with fear-fantasies during the day. The actual happenings of his daily life became distorted in his mind and suggested unreality.

He was obsessed with fears. In the office the typewriter keys looked like animals' teeth; in the midst of his work he was afraid his heart would stop beating; during business conferences he feared he might lose his power of speech and bark like a dog. When walking on the street he was afraid that people would change and look like horses or birds. While driving at night the spare tires of the car in front of him, illuminated by the reflector of his car, appeared to be a huge and frightful face. He feared that he would not recognize the members of his family when he arrived home. At other times, he was haunted by the dread of forgetting who he was, or that he would become blind. When being shaved he was afraid that the barber would cut his face. Nearly all his fears were prominently connected with his eyesight.

His symptoms had existed for about ten years in a mild form. They began to appear when his first child, a son, was born. Then he experienced, for the first time, a feeling that his heart might stop beating. Later he suffered from almost continually blurred vision.

He had left school at the age of seventeen because he was impatient to start a business career and make a great amount of money so that he could retire at about the age of thirty-five and from then on live primarily for pleasure. He had had a younger brother who died at the age of four, when the patient himself was six. The two boys used to play sexual games, which the patient had already been indulging in with other boys and girls. The games usually consisted of sucking each other's breasts and exploring each other's genitalia, especially the girls'. He always wondered why the girls found his "button" (penis) while he could not find theirs.

He remembered that period as having been the happiest of his life, since his father's business trips used to permit his being alone with mother. The late afternoon hours were particularly pleasurable; he sat looking out the window with mother while she told him fairy stories. Most of them were about good fairies, but some were about witches who transformed themselves into animals or human beings or who had the power to change human beings into animals. Naturally, all the fairy stories carried a moral implication. The patient remembered the tale of Pinocchio especially, and his mother's assurance that good little boys got their reward as Pinocchio did. But there was also the other side of the story, when the cricket would whisper constantly in Pinocchio's ear that "bad boys who rebelled against their parents would never get along in the world."

Beneath the pleasures of these early years ran a current of resentment against both parents. He bore little affection for his father partly because he saw him only occasionally, but there was also hatred aroused by the fact that when father was home he came between the little boy and his mother. Moreover, he was responsible for the birth of the younger brother, of whom the patient had been jealous.

His masturbatory activities with both girls and boys continued through adolescence. At the age of ten or eleven he was seduced by a servant girl. She played with his penis and he suckled her breasts. At that time he still adhered to the fantasy that women have only one opening, the anus. He was well developed physically by early adolescence and began to go out with girls. He never had sexual intercourse, but usually on rides or outings he induced the girl to masturbate him. His apparent early development along masculine lines proved to be a pretense and was a result of a disproportionately rapid libidinal growth and slow ego development, both due to his peculiar relationship to his mother.

At the age of eighteen he had his steady girl whom he felt obliged to marry, though his parents opposed it on account of his age. He finally married her when he was not quite twenty-two; she was somewhat older. From the beginning of his marriage he was troubled with ejaculatio praecox, and to satisfy his wife sometimes practised cunnilingus. Very soon after his marriage he began to be troubled with various mild anxieties, all concerning his health. He constantly went to doctors to be examined, and was very much concerned with his stomach and bowel functions. He always entertained the idea of having extramarital sexual relationships, but never came to the point of actually trying. He did make acquaintances, and received a certain amount of gratification through discussing sexual matters with women, or at times petting them, but he always stopped there, usually ending by having an emission. As time went on, he became more and more irritated with his wife. When his first child was born his anxieties became acute.

His anxiety attack was due primarily to his having become a father. (Analogous in a way, to post partem psychoses in women.) He could not bear the realization of his strong early childhood desires to take the father's place, therefore when in actuality he became a parent, he could not enjoy it. His wife was a real substitute mother to him, not only because she was somewhat older, but also because her attitude was motherly. He became obsessed with the idea of leaving his wife, an obsession accompanied by a very strong sense of guilt because it involved the unwelcome child as well as the wife. He was jealous and resentful of his child whom he identified with his dead young brother, whose presence in early childhood he resented because it interfered with having mother's affection all for himself.

His fantasies and constant sexual tension allowed him not a moment's rest. When walking in the street he constantly stared at women, even turning to look at them although he realized that a man in his social position would be an object of criticism if observed in such an activity. Then his vision became blurred and the fear of going blind developed as a protection against looking and desiring.

He disliked coming home from business. The fear of not recognizing the members of his family was indicative of his resentment and strong desire to get away from them. He had the same fear in regard to his parents. The elderly business associates whose noses appeared to change into birdlike beaks were all father representatives, reminding him of his father's supposed sexual superiority and reviving in him a fear of castration. An interesting indication of this strong castration fear was the retention, even until puberty, of the idea that women have only the anal opening. This belief served as a defense against his powerful castration anxieties. By denying any kind of genital in the female, he eliminated even the slightest possibility of the fear of castration.

As an adult his sport diversions were all more or less sexualized, as is often the case with childhood games. Golf was the only activity in which he was superior to his father, and before his anxieties became acute he won many tournaments. After his child was born, however, the smokestacks which were visible from the golf course appeared to be huge animals, the little house on the outskirts of the links a human face; he was seized with an uncontrollable diarrhea and had to rush back to the club house. At the root of all this anxiety was the fear of castration. The outstanding fear, which was that the faces of people might change, had an interesting explanation. It meant that they would change and look angry, since to him normal faces were smiling ones.

A mature man, he was still laboring with the difficulties of his early Oedipus situation. The fears con-

nected with his sexual urges, with the desire to possess
a woman, were directly related to his early childhood desires to possess his mother. In childhood he
had to be good to receive the reward of his mother's
love. Thus the one real danger in childhood, losing
the mother, was warded off by his obedience. As
an adult, the desires for a woman became prominent
once again. These in turn brought anxieties which
emphasized the dangers of adult desires. The woman
(mother) could be both the good fairy and the cruel
witch, and the father, whom his castration fears
concerned, could also be a mighty giant, at times
benevolent, at others severe and punishing. The more
pressing his urge for extra-marital sexual contact
became, the further he had to escape, through his fears,
to ward off the threat of castration by both parents.
All men and women represented his parents. Hence
the world was peopled with menacing, competitive
parental images.

The fear of rivalry with other men, behind which
the moving force was the early feeling of rivalry with
father combined with aggression towards and fear of
him, had to be given opportunity for expression in the
transference relationship. To bring that about and
to help him become a self-reliant, more courageous
person, took nearly three years. Reassurance had to
be freely given at certain periods of analysis. At other
times much frustration and hardship were created, partially because his expectations in the transference situation were not being fulfilled and partially through
suggestions, some aimed at restraining certain childish

activities and others whose object was to make him face situations that provoked anxiety.

In anxiety neuroses there is need of much re-education, because of the patient's strong regressive tendencies and childish fears. (Sometimes re-education must begin with teaching the patient to use a more forward attitude in speech. I pointed out to one patient that his mode of speech indicated his fear of accepting responsibility for his thoughts and feelings. He rarely used the pronoun, "I", instead always tried to discuss things impersonally by using the pronoun, "one". It was apparent that he was actually afraid to associate himself with the material he produced. He also avoided the use of certain words.)

With the above mentioned patient many suggestions had to be given. When he had attained a certain freedom and courage in facing his sexual problem, he interpreted it, as every patient does, as encouragement from the analyst to attempt to have sexual relationships. As this involved creating new conflicts which in the end would provoke guilt feelings, I pointed out the possible difficulties arising from extra-marital relationships, especially since he would not be doing so of his free will but rather under the protection of the analyst, as if he were saying to himself, "the analyst and treatment will take care of all complications". This type of acting out, which is common, must always be interfered with through suggestion. As soon as the analyst recognizes the presence of these tendencies he should try to step in and interpret the patient's plans and their significance, at the same time suggesting their postponement. During the course of treatment I made definite suggestions to control his masturbatory activities and perverse sexual play. The panic on the golf course, which forced him to stop the game and run back to the clubhouse, also had to be handled in a direct manner. Interpretation of the causes of his panic and attacks of diarrhea was not very effective and I therefore suggested that he try to control himself during such anxiety spells and refrain from running back immediately to the men's room. In that way he proved to himself that he was able to control the urge and that no accident would occur. That suggestion provoked a great deal of hostility towards me; it was obviously the feeling carried over from the early childhood training period when he dared not express his aggression against his parents, and therefore repressed it.

At the end of his second year of analysis, when his polymorphous perverse tendencies and need to masturbate had been interpreted, when the origin and meaning of his symptoms had been explained innumerable times and worked through in relation to his marriage, early childhood, and transference relationship, I suggested that he try intercourse without previous fellatio, because of the guilt it engendered. Just as I expected, he soon accused me of interfering with his pleasures and of taking away even the little sexual enjoyment he had. Within a short time, however, he realized that these accusations really referred to early experiences with his parents who so often had interfered with his pleasures. My suggestion to exercise control reactivated his hostility towards his parents and those feelings were transferred to me. Basically, he himself wanted to change his mode of sexual gratification and he finally succeeded in doing so. Instrumental in bringing about that change was his acting out in the analytical situation his long repressed feelings towards his parents.

The patient with the horse phobia [1] was a very intelligent woman of thirty-six, a school teacher, well oriented in psychology and psychoanalytic literature. Her main apprehension was that a horse would fall and break its legs. Whenever she walked on the street, she compulsively thought of the possibility of a horse's falling on the slippery pavement and breaking its legs. It was a source of such anxiety to her that she was compelled to run away whenever she saw horses. A few of her other complaints were fear of tuberculosis of the lungs, a sharp pain under her left shoulder blade, weakness of the whole left side, especially the left arm, shortness of breath, a feeling of pressure on her chest, a steady high blood pressure which puzzled her physicians, and frequent urination (about every two hours, even at night). She was always tired and the doctors considered it a toxic result of her lung trouble. When she came to analysis she had already given up her profession because of this fatigue.

Six years prior to her coming for treatment, coinciding with the time her mother became ill of heart trouble, the patient began to feel vague uneasiness. During her mother's illness she did not complain of any specific ailments. The shortness of breath and the lung symptoms appeared after her mother's death. She then began to visit doctors for her maladies. In

[1] "A Horse Phobia", by S. Lorand, *Psychoanalytic Review,* Vol. XIV, No. 2, 1927.

earlier years she had been operated on for crossed eyes even though she had been able to correct the eye defect herself whenever she made the effort. After her mother's death, in the course of visiting many physicians because of the lung trouble, she began what she termed a love affair with a doctor whose married life she knew to be unhappy. The affair consisted of being petted, to which she submitted, she said, only because she knew the man derived pleasure from it. Actually, she became excited but remained outwardly unresponsive. During this period she developed a vaginal discharge for which she had to be treated locally. The other symptoms also became aggravated and she was suffering from all these manifestations when she came to analysis.

The patient was the younger of two sisters. She felt that in childhood her mother had discriminated against her in favor of the older girl and that she had often been unjustly punished. She had been a bottle baby and could not forgive her mother for the failure to nurse her, feeling that her weakness was due to that deprivation. The mother once explained to the patient that the sister and the two children who had died in infancy had sucked her breasts dry and therefore nothing remained for the patient. (The mother's breasts atrophied.)

During childhood the patient used clever devices to gain the mother's care and attention. When she was six years old she suffered from sunstroke, or at least her malady was thus diagnosed by the family physician, and her mother sat with her all day in the shade of a tree and showed her much tenderness.

After that the patient often reproduced the "sun-stroke" in order to be babied and shown affection. From early childhood on, she overheard arguments between her parents in which the mother accused the father of pursuing other women. This was a justified accusation, and the quarrels ended in divorce when the patient was eleven years old. From that time on she was continually told of the wickedness of men. The mother watched her very closely when she began to have dates with young men and frequently warned her of their "badness". When she was eighteen she broke off her first love affair because of her mother's constant nagging about it. After that episode she was still attracted to men and flirted with them; however, she unconsciously chose men who were either much older than she, married, or so involved that marriage was out of the question.

As soon as she was able to earn a living she supported her mother. During her mother's two year illness she nursed her herself, refusing professional and friendly assistance. She preferred to do everything, even such tasks as injections and night care. Nothing was too difficult or disagreeable; in fact she seems to have enjoyed it, finding in it a dramatic quality which appealed to her.

Concerning her relationship to her father: she had been his favorite. He punished the older sister, but used to pet the patient, buy her candy and take her skating. For a long time he called her "my girl", and when they were out together they walked arm in arm, which made her very proud. She remembered that when she was about five or six years old she used to creep into his bed in the morning, sit on his chest and play. Her memory of pleasurable dreams dates back to a period in which she began to dream of being beaten in place of her sister. She used to pray for a recurrence of these dreams. For a long time after the father left home, she cried a great deal and then began to hate him for being unfaithful to her and to her mother. She never saw him again. Once, after the mother's death, she felt an irresistible longing to search for him. She learned that he was alive, married, and well, and although she had the impulse to communicate with him, for some, to her, inexplicable reason, she did not do so.

The patient was always hostile to her sister. She resented the fact that the sister had preceded her, and she hated her for having sucked the mother's breasts dry so that there was no milk left for the patient. She envied her sister because she went out a great deal and had many friends. The father used to scold her for staying out late and a typical phrase used in his reprimand was: "I will break your legs if you stay out late again." The patient envied not only her sister's freedom but also her beatings, which she considered an expression of attention and care. After the divorce, the sister also left home and both mother and patient were glad to see her go.

In the first week of analysis she brought in the following dream:

"I am in a crowd on a street corner. A dead cat is in my arms. I revive it . . . but something is wrong with the cat, as if its hemispheres (of the brain) were cut out. Something is wrong with the semi-circular canals. I cannot cross the street. There are horses there and I am afraid something will happen to them."

This dream contains the nucleus of the neurosis in condensed form. It not only indicates her castration fears, but relates it clearly and directly to her horse phobia. The cat (vagina) is deprived of its hemispheres (testicles) and something is wrong with the semi-circular canals (also vagina). She dares not cross the street (to solve her problem) because she fears that something will happen to the horse (her masculinity).

The following is one of her many castration dreams:

"I am holding a cat in my arms. Two elephants are approaching. I am afraid the elephant will hurt the cat."

Her associations to this dream were: "I am afraid to marry. The hymen will be hurt. A friend of mine went to a physician to have it broken artificially. My mother said that father 'went into her' in two nights and she could never forgive him for it." (The elephant is a characteristic masculine symbol not only because it is a big animal but also because of its trunk.)

The patient considered analysis a castration and her aggressive attitude toward me in the first part of treatment was really a protection against falling in love, against developing a transference, which would mean giving up her masculinity (being castrated).

The following dream is an illustration of her fear and defense:

"I have a long stick in my hand. Somebody pares it with a knife so that it becomes smaller and smaller and only a little piece of it remains. I am pursued. It is a life and death chase. I think, 'I shall escape', but this thought also comes, 'If that little piece gets into the hands of my enemy I'm lost.' "

She awoke with anxiety, repeating the words "escape, escape". (The diminishing stick is a phallic symbol; paring it is equated with castration and the small piece which remains is the clitoris in which she retained her masculinity.) Her fear of relinquishing her masculinity was based on her dread of the acceptance of femininity and the inferiority which it signified to her. Around this fear her whole conflict was built. At first she was unwilling to accept the idea of not having a penis, of being a girl, which in her unconscious equalled castration. Her penis-envy derived from this conflict and castration tendencies were directed against every man as was often revealed in her dreams.

Another castration dream deals directly with the analyst:

"You are Buddha, sitting on my breast. A violent defloration follows. I throw you down on the floor and you lie there with a bloody penis."

(She often said I was the Mysterious One sitting behind her, whose presence she felt only by the cigar smoke.) The meaning of her symptom, shortness of breath was clarified by her associations to this dream. I have already mentioned that as a child she used to sit on her father's chest; that was really a form of childish masturbation. Her anxiety which expressed itself in shortness of breath, could be interpreted as the wish for this act in reversed positions; that is, the wish for direct incest from which she is protecting herself by anxiety. The breathing difficulty is also the punishment for the wish. Buddha represents the Almighty Father (analyst) whom she is castrating.

The foregoing dreams and associations illustrated her castration tendencies, penis-envy and strong adherence to masculine tendencies. All were expressed in her unconscious by the fantasy of retaining a penis, which was represented by the clitoris. Necessarily, then, there must also be a castration fear relating to the retained penis. And, actually, her horse phobia was a pure expression of the castration fear. In connection with the case of "Little Hans", in *Inhibition, Symptom and Anxiety,* Freud established that anxiety is a signal to the ego of danger of castration. The animal phobia itself is an emotional reaction of the ego to the danger of castration. In this case the mechanism of the neurosis is somewhat different from that of "Little Hans" but the theme is essentially the same.

In the first dream her castration fear was connected with the horse phobia. Other dreams repeatedly brought the phobia to the surface:

"Two horses draw a cab. I hit the left horse; it falls into a ditch. I am frightened, thinking it

is hurt. But the horse gets up and goes to the right
side and looks at me. It is not hurt."

Her associations: the horses are her parents; the left
horse is father who "went the wrong way" (chasing
other women).

Another dream:

"I am riding down a curved path in a bus drawn
by horses. A man in the shadow drives the horses.
I am afraid of an accident."

The association to this dream was an "accident" her
mother once told her of, in which her brutal husband
drove her over rough roads in order to produce a mis-
carriage. The patient often thought that she too
might have died in the uterus in the same way as that
unborn child. The thought expressed a deep castration fear (also, identification with her mother).

In the horse phobia, the horse really represents the
patient herself, through identification with both parents. The identification is exemplified in these dreams:

"Two horses are driven on a highway. They are
tired, can scarcely pull, and fall every few moments.
The driver is intoxicated—he doesn't care."

The associations are: The two horses are she and her
mother, thrown into difficulty by the father's behavior.
The mother often used to say: "All my life I have
worked like a horse." In connection with this dream,
the patient said: "My mother had a sad face. I have
a long sad face like a horse and I have to bear the
burden of life."

Another:

"A fat man is whipping a horse with a stick because the horse will not lie down. At once the horse changes into a man who is suffering terribly. His agony is written on his face, and he holds his hand on a spot on his back where the pain is most intense. (It is the same spot where I feel my pains.) I say to the driver, 'Why don't you let him stand upright if he wants to?' The driver answers, 'You are right!' "

The drunken driver is the analyst who makes her lie down on the couch. (She often voiced objections to this position.) Symbolically the reclining position makes her a woman, against which she unconsciously protests. The man who was transformed from a horse is the patient; the identification of the sore spot on his back with her own pain indicates this. The wish is to stand up, to get the analyst's permission to get up; in other words, to retain her masculinity and not be forced to change.

She identifies herself with a horse in another dream:

"I see a horse and someone is forcing his mouth open and tries to push a stick into it. I resent it."

The interpretation is obviously forced coitus.

The fear that horses will break their legs means, at the deepest level, a death wish against the father on whose chest she used to ride, and also expresses a castration wish directed against men in general. Because of her feeling of guilt resulting from the death wish, she punishes herself by reversing the situation.

The death wish is turned against herself, and she therefore becomes the horse (the father) and fears breaking her legs. The anxiety that the horse will break its legs then represents the fear of losing her penis (clitoris erotism), losing her hymen, falling (morally), which related to her prostitution fantasies.

Her fear of analysis and her resistance to it, as already mentioned, was also a protection against castration. All the resentment she expressed in analysis had been engendered by her parents. At first she had violent day dreams in which she tortured the therapist. These gave place little by little to tender feelings, and she slowly began to have fantasies of being in love with the analyst and of having a child by him. That corresponded to her childhood fantasy of having a baby by her father. Sexual fantasies about the analyst repeatedly came to her mind and finally her old castration fear openly showed itself to be a *wish for* castration. I shall illustrate this by one of her dreams:

"I am lying in bed. I stretch my hand out to the lamp; the burner explodes and I am wounded. I have a hole in my forehead. I pull down my hat to cover the hole, but notice that the blood stains the band on my hat. I go to a doctor for treatment. He is a Jew, but kind and nice."

The first association to this dream was: "I am going to you to stop my bleeding." Further associations brought out the latent content. The lamp exploding and wounding her she connected with intercourse and bleeding which referred to her wish for castration.

Further, being cared for by me, having me stop her bleeding expressed her wish for a cessation of her menses, i.e., being pregnant. In this connection it is necessary to mention that her need for frequent urination, which was one of her symptoms, was related to pregnancy fantasies. At the age of sixteen, against her mother's wish, she went for a ride with a boy. She became sexually excited, wanted to urinate but was ashamed to say anything and retained her urine for many hours, until she returned home. Her tendency to frequent urination dated from this episode. Her associations to this dream indicated that she equated retention of urine with pregnancy and had to reassure herself that her bladder, which equalled uterus to the unconscious, was not distended. Urination was also a form of masturbation for her.

Fantasies of anal childbirth were also present. The feces represented child and penis. One of her favorite occupations was to collect manure from the street to fertilize her garden (Mother Earth).

As the repressed tender feelings were released and came to the surface, a yearning for her mother became frequent. She sometimes behaved like a helpless child —cried easily, lamented the fact that she was alone in the world, recalled her childhood miseries, and often complained that she was hungry during the analytic hour. She established the habit of drinking a bottle of milk every morning. During the night she arose and sucked an orange. When she left the analyst's office she bought candy and sucked it, because, she said, she wanted to have some sweetness in life since she had experienced so much misery. She wanted to be the breast-child to compensate for her childhood deprivation. Many of her dreams showed wishes connected with the breast. The following is an example:

"My mother is preparing the table for dinner. There is a nice pitcher which she carelessly breaks. I reproach her angrily but when she bursts into tears I cry with her, embrace her and feel her flesh soft in my hands as I never felt it before."

Her associations to this dream: she resents not having had mother's breasts and reproaches her for being the cause of father's leaving home. Breaking the pitcher means denial of the breast and it also represents the penis. If mother had not been so argumentative and cold sexually, father would not have left home. In connection with this dream she said: "I am a weakling not only because I was not breast-fed but because I am not a love child (not conceived in love). Mother was cold; how then can I be loving?" It must be remembered that being bottle-fed was one of her deep-rooted traumas which prevented her from developing a good identification with the mother.

Another dream from the same period of analysis ran as follows:

"I am carrying a crippled child five or six years old. It talks but I do not understand it. I am going to a crippled children's home. There is a girl with a baby in her arms. She calls me and spreads the baby's legs apart. I see that it is a girl, and I see the pubic hair on the genitals. Then I notice that one leg is shorter than the other. She shows me that the baby has a poorly developed penis and testicles.   The penis is flat instead of round and it is red.   The girl says that the baby is not sexually mature.   The child has herpes on the lips and it occurs to me that it has lues."

When the patient had this dream, she had had herpes on her lips for three days.   The baby in the dream is the patient herself, as her associations proved.   She is at the crossroads and must decide whether to remain where she is or to change and proceed in another direction.   During this period which was one of great struggle, she stopped masturbating and changed her sleeping position to side or back.   (Formerly she was unable to sleep in any position other than on her stomach).   She later resumed masturbation, lying on her back, and with this change came her desire for intercourse.   The wish to accept the feminine role is manifest in the following dream:

First part: "There is an amphitheater.   I am dancing with a crowd of dancers, men and girls. They throw me down.   I lie on my stomach and a Chinese girl puts her foot on my back.   I feel it distinctly."

Second part: "I am on a stage.   I consider throwing the girl off my back, but I think, 'That will kill her.'   So I push her down and start to dance with a man.   He throws me down on my back and I think, 'Let's have intercourse.'   But in order to make the scene more spectacular he is transformed into a Negro.   The mixed color will make a nicer performance.   He is touching my vagina with his penis; I have an orgasm."

When she awoke, her first thought was: "I certainly will not tell this dream to the analyst."

The first part refers to the patient's past situation, the second to the present. Originally she lay on her stomach, in which position she masturbated, having the fantasy of being a man. Then she gave up that position. In the second part of her dream she starts to dance with a man, lies under him and the dance ends in a climax produced by the touch of his penis. The second part represented her real wish. The Negro dancer indicates her desire to have intercourse with the analyst, who appeared as a Negro in her dreams because of his complexion which seemed very dark to the patient who was exceedingly fair. Further, she put Jews and Negroes in the same category, and although she did not know my religion, Freud was Jewish, psychoanalysis was therefore a Jewish science and all analysts Jews.

At the time that we discussed the termination of analysis she cried bitterly and came to the next analytic hour with this dream:

"I am in front of a hospital. It is after the war between Europe and America. I see a soldier with a wooden mask on his head in which there are holes for the mouth, nose and eyes. I think, 'What is life to him?' Then another soldier appears, a tall blonde fellow who has no arms. He walks quietly in the sunshine. I think, 'At least he can walk,' and I also walk away in the sunshine."

Both soldiers are the patient. The first represented her current attitude, walking about with a wooden mask on her face (her blue eyes and long face were practically devoid of expression). The second soldier signified her wish to resign herself to life without sex (the arms symbolizing both a penis and masturbation.) The next day she reported that when she returned home after the analytic hour she found that she was menstruating. Apparently it had begun during the analytic hour without the customary warnings several days ahead. She had talked of "jus primae noctis" and symbolically accomplished the act by starting her menstruation in the analyst's office.

The same day she had another interesting experience. (This was during the last few days of analysis.) While lying in bed, she felt as if the left side of her body, including her arm and leg, had grown to gigantic proportions and she had to test the hallucination by actually feeling the various parts of her body. She explained it as an over-compensation for "my former weak and sick left side." (All her conversion symptoms were on the left side.) She remembered having had similar sensations once when her mother was ill. At that time she felt as if her head were swollen and doubled in size. Both these hallucinations were connected with the variations of her ego feelings, the transition from a depressive and self-depreciatory stage to an optimistic and self-confident one. She stated that during the period of her mother's illness everything seemed like play. She received unconscious gratification from caring for her, and the feeling that her head was swelling was the symbolic expression of her pride (swelled head) at being able to bear the responsibilities just as a man would have. It was also a symbolic expression of the wish to be a man, having a penis through upward displacement. Just as, at the close of analysis, her confidence in the future expressed itself in the hypnagogic hallucination of swelling of the left side.

To summarize this abbreviated history: Her fair adjustment up to the time of her mother's death can be explained by the mechanism of double identification. Primary identification with the mother had taken place, but there was stronger identification with the father, which developed later. Through the latter identification she replaced the father in fantasy, and in reality replaced him by supporting and helping her mother until her death.

After her mother's death all the conflicts became active and the resultant feeling of illness forced her to seek help of doctors, with one of whom she began a one-sided, incomplete sexual affair. She was unable to fully enjoy the relationship because the doctor was a father substitute (among other similarities he was unhappily married), and the affair mobilized the old Oedipus conflicts, causing a return of childhood ambivalence. Hence, the old guilt feeling was also reactivated and it resulted in frigidity. The frustrated excitement in this love affair accumulated and caused the anxiety preparedness on which foundation the other symptoms developed. Her phobia represented the protection of the ego against the libidinal strivings.

The phobia is also the punishment for the unconscious incest wish. As always, the horse is a symbol for the father. The fear that something will happen to the horse—"It may break its legs," is, in the first place, a castration wish against the father (death

wishes). It also represents her wish for sexual intercourse, being hurt, deflorated. The patient's childhood fantasy of being beaten by the father, proves
that the fear of the breaking of legs expressed an
unconscious wish for something pleasurable. She was
a witness of her sister's beatings and heard her father's
oft-reiterated phrase: "I will break your legs".

In *A Child Is Being Beaten*, Freud gave the first
explanation of this fantasy, which is common in children. He explained its development in three phases.
The child's fantasies are:

1. Father is beating a child.
2. Father beats a child whom I hate (he loves only
me).
3. I am beaten by father (masochistic character).
In the foregoing case the fantasy starts at the second
phase. "Father beats older sister whom I dislike,
he loves me", which was the situation in reality. The
desire to be beaten also represents her wish for punishment for the incestuous love.

The nucleus of the neurosis was formed from the
combination of castration tendencies against men and
flight from womanhood, which at the deepest level
was flight from incest, the desire for which deserved
punishment. Every one of her conversion symptoms
had a special symbolic value through her identification
with one or the other parent. The pains at the left
side of her body were partly due to identification with
her mother, who suffered with backaches. One day
she came into her mother's room just as the mother
had an attack of shortness of breath. At that moment
she felt the pressure around her breast for the first

time. The symptom of shortness of breath, which produced in the patient exaggerated fear of tuberculosis of the lungs, was the same symptom from which her mother had suffered. It may also have meant as previously stated a repressed wish for intercourse, for she described the symptom with the words: "As if someone were sitting on my chest", a reversal of childhood play in which she sat on her father's chest. The symptom of frequent urination, as was explained before, was partially a substitute for masturbation and also served as an assurance that she was not pregnant. (Bladder equalling uterus).

At certain periods it became necessary to make suggestions to the patient which created temporary tension and resistance, and were rather difficult tasks to carry out. First, the suggestion to face her phobia of crossing the street or going out into the street had to be given, but at a time when her positive transference was well established. At this stage of her treatment I knew that if given the choice of accepting or rejecting a suggestion, she would carry it out and the resistance thus created could be resolved. I emphasize suggestion and not command or restriction because the latter two contain the danger of the patient's accepting them only as tools with which to later defy the analyst. Some suggestions given and carried out were: to try to control frequent urination during the day and to check masturbation. Although she understood the object of these suggestions, whenever she felt contrary and hostile in analysis, she masturbated; not only for the sake of pleasure, but also to express defiance and to inhibit progress, thus to nullify the analyst's efforts to effect a change in her.

She commenced her treatment with criticism of analysis and denial that her symptoms had any sexual significance or implications. Quite early in treatment she declared that to her analysis was a game which she wanted to win by proving that the therapist was mistaken about the meaning of her symptoms. This wish to prove the therapist in error expressed her attitude toward men in general. Because she felt that the woman's role in a sex relationship was one of slavery, she endeavored to justify her consequent avoidance of men on the score that they were inferior in intelligence and ability and completely lacking in appreciation of women. The basis of that concept was her father's attitude to her mother.

During the first part of her analysis, the aggression and anxiety which were a defense against her castration fear, came to the surface and grew progressively stronger. Later, when positive feelings for the analyst began to arise, the aggression and anxiety slowly subsided and were replaced by moodiness and feelings of frustration. She behaved like a child, imploring help, love, guidance, and the like. A detailed working through of the origin and development of these feelings enabled her to achieve a gradual acceptance of femininity, which of course involved the giving up of her masculine characteristics. She became consistently stronger, but still slipped back at times to the former childish dependence upon the analyst, involving the desire to have a sexual relationship with him, which would have meant to her an expression of his love. During these setbacks she cried bitterly, accused the analyst of having taken away her pride, of having made a little child of her so that she could no longer go out into the world on her own resources. Her former symptoms, which otherwise had been completely absent for a long period, reappeared on those occasions to challenge the results of therapy. However, due to her actual progress and the degree of independence she had achieved by that time, such flare-ups of old symptoms and behavior were of very short duration.

My suggestions to this patient were made in the manner in which Freud used them originally and on which Ferenczi later elaborated, referring to their use as "active technique". Not much space will be devoted to reviewing the various aspects of so-called active therapy which is connected with the name of Ferenczi. It is important to know, however, that his original object was the stimulation of progress in patients whose analysis seemed to be at a standstill. The function of the active measure is to bring to the surface the instinctual drive which is hidden by the symptom. The patient is induced to face a situation which creates anxiety or frustration. His reactions to it expose the intensity of the instinctual drive and thus provide further material for analysis.

At the International Psychoanalytic Congress of 1920 at the Hague, Ferenczi described the indications for active therapy and methods of application. He emphasized its use in the sphere of analysis of sexual habits, especially in regard to anal and urethral activities which have proved to be symptom manifestations of infantile pre-genital fixations. By following suggestions to control habits of this type (which are of a masturbatory nature) sexual tension is created and can then be directed towards genital gratification.

Freud himself applied active technique with some types of patients.

The analyst's experience and intuition are his only guides in determining whether and when to use active measures. Sometimes he must be positive in his attitude and suggestions and yet he will not be active in the sense that most beginning analysts understand the term; in other words, he does not command or exert pressure. He makes the patient understand that he is asked to try to follow suggestions because they will facilitate a change to more normal behavior, which the patient himself wants to achieve.

No therapist can get along without using some form of active therapy. But if the analyst interferes because of his own irritation or annoyance with the patient's behavior, such "activity" can bring about critical phases in the analysis and even cause the patient to discontinue treatment.

In the treatment of certain neuroses, Ferenczi's devices are not only helpful, but indispensable. That is especially true of the analysis of character difficulties, in connection with which one hears so much about "negative therapeutic reactions".

Chapter IV

SEXUAL DIFFICULTIES IN
THE MALE

In the analysis of various types of neuroses, one finds neurotic symptoms and attitudes relating to the patient's sexual behavior, which must be corrected in the course of treatment. In some cases the sexual difficulties are most prominent, and in many instances are the reason for seeking treatment. Most common are sexual impotence in the male and frigidity in the female. For the present we shall concern ourselves only with the problem of male impotence. The term covers varying degrees of difficulty which range from complete impotence to occasional disturbances and includes ejaculatio praecox, masturbatory intercourse, and various perverse tendencies and practices.

As a rule psychic impotence is amenable to psychoanalytic treatment and has a good prognosis, especially in the hysterical type of patient. It should be treated as a conversion hysterical symptom, which is not difficult to eliminate. In all cases of sexual difficulty, various other neurotic symptoms complicate the picture, but the outstanding symptoms pertain to sexual life.

As analysis progresses, it will become increasingly obvious that the patient cannot fulfill his pleasure aim because he is unable to face the dangers which sex represents for him. These dangers seem formidable because he views and feels them with the intensity of his childhood reaction. To put it briefly, his castration anxiety overcomes his pleasure drive.

In their unconscious these patients are overwhelmed with fear that is charged with all its childhood intensity. The key to the problem of male impotence and female frigidity lies in Freud's discovery of infantile sexuality. The task of analysis is to free the patient of his early incestuous attachment, by first making him accept that early attachment, and then leading him via the transference relationship, to other objects which both satisfy and suit his adult needs. In the analysis of sexual difficulties there are many opportunities for observing how the defense mechanisms constantly create resistance to the progress of the treatment and aim at counteracting the analyst's effort to help the patient to a more mature attitude toward sex. All the defenses go into the service of defending the ego against the id drives. The analyst's success depends upon his resolving those defenses and reducing the threats of the superego by making the patient face both the drives which were hitherto unconscious and also his superego (his own moralistic censor). He will thus learn to be less afraid of them and not feel the need to run away.

The very best advice I can give for success with such cases is: Always think of the patient as a fearful, badly behaved child. Think of him as having to grow up under the analyst's tutelage and guidance. Great tact is required to avoid frightening such patients and tolerance to resist becoming tired and annoyed with their abuse and aggression.

The progress of analysis depends largely upon the analyst's attitude. Therefore from the very beginning, one must be careful not to appear to be a moralistic censor, not to sound as if accusing or pronouncing a sentence upon the patient for his childish sexuality or perverse tendencies. The analyst can very easily lead the patient to feel that he is abnormal and thus frighten him away from analysis. I have met a number of patients who were told in their starting period of analysis that they were perverts or homosexuals. Naturally, they were terrified and withdrew from treatment.

The analyst may see in the patient's sexual practices some unconscious homo-sexuality or perverse manifestations. However, the patient not having had overt homosexual experience, cannot be called homosexual. I always make it a point to explain to the patient who accuses himself of being homosexual, that since he has had neither overt homosexual relationships nor any such conscious desires, he cannot be homosexual. True, he may have dreams with homosexual content, or unconscious desires of being supported, advised, loved by a male, just as a little boy wants those things from his father, but his real sexual desires are hetero-sexual. If that were not the case and the stronger pull were toward his own sex, he would have followed that line of development.

With a detailed explanation like the foregoing, I include a description and discussion of the early biological and psychological development of the child, not omitting the factor of universal bisexuality. Such explanations greatly further the patient's progress; they help him understand his early attachments and frustrations, and in addition have the effect of promoting the transference relationship.

All patients with sexual difficulties indulge in childhood forms of gratification, such as masturbation, through which they partially satisfy their sexual urges. They thus avoid being very deeply disturbed by sexual drives and hence temporarily escape the need for adult sexual practices.

Some of these cases come for treatment because of their many neurotic symptoms, or because of general social difficulties: feelings of inferiority, shyness, dissatisfaction, and unhappiness, but it very soon becomes apparent that these symptoms are all due to an inadequate sexual life.

A male patient came for treatment because he felt restless and unhappy. Before long his conversation narrowed down to straight complaints about his wife: she managed the home and children badly, she nagged him constantly and made him feel that he was responsible for all the difficulties at home because of his sexual inadequacy. It is interesting to note that he thought he was oversexed, a belief which was confirmed by physicians whom he consulted about the problem. He gave a history of abstinence up to his marriage, although he was attractive to women and many tried to seduce him during his college years. He was a good dancer and very sociable but always apprehensive of unpleasantness. On his honeymoon, he was "extraordinarily potent", but could not achieve an orgasm. Later that condition improved so that after prolonged intercourse he could ejaculate.

Very early in analysis he became impotent intermittently. It always occurred when he became aware of annoyance and irritations caused by his wife which he did not discuss with her, or when he became angry with his colleagues and did not try to work out the annoying situation with them.

It was quite an achievement for him to be able to acknowledge thoughts and fantasies about other women. He fought these fantasies because they conflicted with his upbringing and religious education, but his improvement in analysis definitely started with his acceptance of such fantasies without fear. To bring him to that point I had to give the equivalent of a course in the physiology and psychology of sex. It proved to be an arduous task although he was an intelligent person with college training. His seeming ignorance should give some idea of the depth of the repression which had to be broken to make him amenable to analytical therapy.

This patient's "hypersexuality" served amongst other functions as a cover for imperfections and lack of self-confidence. Strong sadism and impulsiveness were hidden behind various anxieties and good behavior. For instance, he was in great fear of being near a gun or carrying one. (He used to live on a farm where hunting was a favored pastime, but he never participated.) He was considered a reckless driver, but never had an accident. He always drove "like mad" and had to be the first to start after a halt for a traffic light. Defiance of law, policemen and rules was expressed in his behavior at the wheel and in this way only, did he give vent to his aggression. His prolonged erections proved to be a defense against the vagina. He had a deep unconscious fear of the vagina "dentata". His erect penis represented a weapon with

which he could protect himself. Ejaculation meant
loss of his weapon and consequent inability to fight
the vagina. In order to maintain his erection he fantasied all kinds of sexual scenes with various women.
When he began to sense the approach of an orgasm
he changed the image, starting all over again with a
new woman, thus prolonging the erection. Later he
did not even reach an orgasm. He simply continued
the act until his wife tired of it, or had an orgasm.
In the advanced stages of analysis, many dreams about
the female penis revealed his basic castration fear. It
was due to a strong Oedipus fixation, intensified by
actual sexual play with his sisters in childhood. At
the time he was constantly fearful of being caught,
but also felt defiant at the thought of such interference
from his parents. Through following my suggestion
to stop this masturbatory intercourse, he slowly reduced
the number of images involved in his fantasies, bringing about an orgasm in a shorter time. He could not,
however, at that stage, completely give up thinking
of another woman when having intercourse with his
wife.

Not having an orgasm meant withholding something from his wife, denying her his valuable semen
which to him was a symbol of money. Furthermore
he did not want to give her children although he himself desired them very much.

In all patients whose sexual difficulties are prominent various perverse tendencies or fantasies manifest
themselves. The degree of sexual difficulty can be
determined by the type, frequency, and intensity of
the fantasies and the extent of their preoccupation
with perversions. It is imperative that the analyst

discuss in detail with the patient the meaning of the fantasies and perverse forms of gratification.

In cases of impotence and other sexual problems in male and female, the object-relationship is weak. To a large degree it is on the pre-genital level; as a result of the early childhood disappointment in the relationship with the parent of the opposite sex, fundamental distrust has been carried over to adult life. This distrust becomes, in adult life, a barrier against strong emotional ties and in the neurotic person it serves as a protection against the disappointment and pain of a possible rejection by the beloved person. Plainly the purpose of the distrust is to avoid a repetition of the early traumatic experience.

The following case gives some understanding of the many factors involved in this problem. A young man in his middle twenties came for treatment because of a urinary problem. At times he found it difficult to hold his urine, and on other occasions he could not decide whether or not he needed to urinate. He would feel the urge but upon leaving the room it would disappear. This uncertainty and weak control became aggravated to the extent that he was afraid to mingle with people or make a date with a girl. He was embarrassed at the possibility of people's attention being focussed on his going to the bathroom if he left the room.

This urinary difficulty supposedly was his sole complaint and reason for coming to analysis. He did not consider himself impotent sexually because he had made a few attempts which he considered to be successful, and believed that at his age he was not supposed to be more active sexually. It was clear from the beginning of treatment that his sexual functioning was not mature. He obtained sexual gratification chiefly through heavy petting; what he liked most was kissing girls' breasts. Several girls tried to seduce him but he attempted coitus only twice, both times ending in ejaculatio praecox, which he considered successful intercourse.

The urinary problem was caused by deep castration fear and was the result of a regression to urinary activities of early childhood. It was protection against getting into more serious trouble sexually, and preoccupation with the problem of urination was a substitute for preoccupation with heterosexual activity. This type of gratification carried with it its own punishment, and in the deepest layer of his unconscious it expressed a desire for exhibitionism, i.e. his desire to attract attention to his genitals. It is interesting to note that he was more embarrassed in the company of men than he was with women. This was due to the unconscious homosexual attachment to his father, and guilt because of it.

In his early childhood he had been very much afraid of his father who was a morose business man, very strict and severe with his wife as well as with the children. The patient was acutely jealous of his older brother and had strong feelings of hostility towards him. The older brother was identified in his mind with his father and the patient succeeded in his endeavor to excel him in intellectual attainments, but in relations with women he felt inferior to him.

His relationship to his mother was marked by strong feelings of tenderness and great conscious attachment. He had always felt that she was in the right when there were arguments between her and his father. When as a child the patient was bullied by his older brother, he always ran to her for protection. He actually received more of his mother's attention in childhood than did his brother because he was a weak child and when he was not quite a year old, he had some kidney trouble. This he learned from overhearing family conversations.

As in every case of sexual impotence, he could not achieve an adult mode of genital functioning because of castration fear, which was bound up with early strong attachments to, and fears of parents. His strong exhibitionistic tendencies carried sadistic impulses; sexual intercourse itself was thought of by him as a strongly sadistic action. Overhearing parental sexual intimacies added to his castration anxieties. He also knew that his mother had had several abortions and that they had endangered her life. This made an even deeper impression on him: "A man may kill a woman with sex." Thus his unconscious defenses against having relations with women were strengthened.

The most difficult problem in his analysis was to make him perceive, understand and externalise his long-repressed aggression and thus reduce his fear and feeling of inferiority; for, his various symptoms, bound up as they were with his sexual difficulties, colored his general behavior and consequently affected his social life. Analysis had not only to rid him of his symptoms, but also to help him feel and act differently in all situations.

For instance: he had to work in one office with his father and several relatives, a situation he disliked intensely. Often before he had begun analytic treatment he contemplated changing to another job, but never had the courage to face the family criticism such a step would have evoked. During his analysis, the thought of changing jobs and even changing his occupation, became still more tempting and several times nearly had the effect of interrupting his treatment. It was difficult for him to face the realization, to which analysis had brought him, that his desire to change jobs was an expression of an attempt to run away from reality.

Another reason for staying in his father's office, besides dread of family criticism, was fear that his urination compulsion would disturb him on another job. That same uncertainty kept him in analysis which he wanted to terminate. He, of course, accused me of keeping him at his job and exposing him to disturbances which he felt were due to working under the scrutiny of father and relatives. All his hostility and aggression were directed to me for many months and this ventilation of his negative feelings in the transference situation was tremendously helpful in effecting his cure. During this period his need for frequent urination, which for a long time had subsided, returned with renewed vigor in the analytic sessions. He frequently had to interrupt the hour and hasten to the bathroom.

This return of the symptom was a symbolic expression of his dissatisfaction with analysis and disappointment in me. With it he indicated his aggression, showing me that the treatment, instead of helping, was aggravating his condition; (he considered the period when the symptom subsided to be the time when he was cured) and the return of the symptom he emphatically attributed to my mishandling of his case. It was also an expression of his exhibitionistic tendencies; making me aware of his urination was a symbolic way of showing me his penis, and lastly, urination also meant active masturbation in my presence ("right in my parent's face") with less fear than he had experienced in childhood. In addition, frequent urination carried the unconscious meaning of producing a great amount of urine, which, in a sense meant a bigger penis than his father's or older brother's. He connected the ability to produce urine with the size of the penis.

In the advanced stage of analysis he had recurrent dreams about intercourse, awakening with the feeling that he was having a seminal emission and actually just stopping himself from urinating. He also had a dream about urinating and lying in the nice, warm urine, but did not wet himself as he had done between the ages of six and nine.

The actual re-living of early emotional experiences in the transference relationship is of especially great importance in cases where sexual difficulties are outstanding symptoms. In the positive transference relationship, the analyst will be expected to be more understanding, more dependable and a more helpful parent than the patient's childhood experiences made his parents appear to him. In the negative phase, the patient must be given the opportunity to express his repressed feelings, provoked in childhood by the frustrations imposed by parents and by their real or supposed negligence and cruelty. These feelings will be expressed as a reaction to fancied mistreatment on the part of the analyst. All patients of this type become very abusive and aggressive. The analyst's narcissism is put to the test and he is liable to be provoked to impatience and harshness. At this point it is appropriate to refer again to the suggestion to think of the patient as a helpless child. Sexual difficulties are the most fruitful task for psychoanalytic therapy if they are handled with benevolence, understanding, and empathy.

This patient's strong infantile regression was partly due to the attention he had received from his mother in connection with his early kidney ailment. His strong feelings of rivalry which dated back to the Oedipus period, were expressed in his urethral eroticism. Various suggestions were made to him: he was asked to check masturbatory play, to refrain from acting out his hostility against his father and brother, and to eliminate the heavy petting which served to check the development of deeper sexual feeling for women. He was also advised to control his substitute gratifications: urinary and bowel preoccupations which involved frequent trips to the toilet. Urination substituted at times for orgasm, the urine representing semen. Thus he avoided impregnating a woman, and thus allayed one of his unconscious fears. His sexual desires were strongly sadistic and he tried to escape from them by getting rid of sexual tension through urination. The fear of "vagina dentata" was apparent in this patient also and basic defenses were directed against that castration threat.

All these unconscious tendencies in the deepest sense expressed the wish to be a little boy who has no adult sexual expression and no concern with penis or vagina, whose only desire is to be loved, to have oral pleasures (breast), and in whom genital pleasures go no further than urination.

The next case I reported eleven years ago.[1] The patient has been well since then. I believe it is a good illustration of what can be accomplished with proper handling.

This patient sought treatment for his sexual difficulties. At the time he began analysis, he was in his early thirties and both parents had been dead for a number of years. Concern about his very unsatisfactory sexual life was preventing adequate concentration on his work. Also, he harbored fears of physical illness and fear of criticism. But above all he feared that he would be unable to carry out his sexual relationships properly and that women would not think well of him. He had never been able to get along easily with them; only in the preceding few years had he developed closer relationships with a number of women, with whom he attempted sexual intercourse, sometimes with a fair degree of success.

He was always afraid of being left by his female friends, because he felt inferior to other men with whom they might have had sex relations. When such fears of losing his partner arose, he made every effort to retain her friendship. For example, he once forsook an excellent business opportunity in one state to rush back to the state where his friend lived, and from there followed her to a third state, because of an entirely groundless fear of losing her.

[1] "A Note on the Psychology of the Inventor," by S. Lorand, *Psychoanalytic Quarterly*, Vol. III, 1934.

Both parents had been away a great deal, his mother had been in business and his father had travelled extensively. He at times had admired his father for his achievements but always had feared him. To his mother, however, he had retained his attachment despite her daily absence from home. At school he had excelled in all subjects, and had been set up as an example to the other students.

His fantasies, which started at an early age, played an important role in his sexual life. Indulging in various perversions and fantasying about them gave him great pleasure. These fantasies were mostly of an exhibitionistic nature. In them he conceived of various methods of masturbation. He used to slide down the bannisters and he remembers the pleasurable sensations he experienced along with the pain and pressure in the genital region. He suffered from worms for which his mother administered enemas. Anticipating them was a source of pleasure as well as of anxiety.

From childhood to early puberty he slept in his parents' bedroom. At the age of twelve, when he slept with his mother one night, she discovered him in the act of masturbating and warned him of its dangers. Around that time he also slept with a male cousin with whom he used to discuss sexual intercourse although he was afraid his mother might overhear them. During his puberty period his masturbation practices were of the same nature as in early childhood: pressing his penis against various objects like lamp posts, sliding posts in the gymnasium, or toilet seats. It is interesting that he could never remember having had an erection when masturbating. At puberty he overheard the intercourse of his parents and his fantasies about it gave him great pleasure. Another childhood fantasy that he remembered concerned the possibility of his changing into a woman.

At the age of thirteen, when he slept in his parents' bedroom on a couch, he had his first seminal emission. He became panic stricken because he thought that the semen was bloody and would leave marks on his bedding. From then on he masturbated more frequently, with a mounting desire to experience pleasure. He invented different methods to increase the pleasure. When he was alone in the house, and he often was, he had two objectives which were frequently combined: either to masturbate or to find something sweet to eat. He would drink milk, then smear some on his penis and then masturbate in a position that would cause the semen to fall on his face. At other times he ate chocolate and smeared some on his penis. He inserted violin strings in his urethra for stimulation. While fantasying about girls using them, he inserted candles in his rectum. He also inserted glass tubes, which were obtained from his chemical experiments.

At the age of sixteen he was taken to a prostitute by his brother. He tried intercourse, but it was a failure. Ten years later he tried again, this time with success. The circumstances were rather curious. It was done on a park bench on a cold winter night and he was constantly preoccupied with the fear of being attacked or killed or both. (In the newspapers he had read about such attacks upon couples in the park.)

From then on, whenever he indulged in sexual activity there was always accompanying fear.

His older brother's sexual successes made the patient feel very inferior. He tried to compensate for it through superiority in intellectual matters, and during the time of his analysis his brother had become dependent on him for financial aid.

In all his sexual relationships the patient practised cunnilingus because he feared the girl would leave him, and he believed that to maintain the attachment, he had to excite and gratify her in that manner. Some of his sexual partners reproached him for insisting on such perverse practices. The reproach intensified his fear of losing the girl, but at the same time it increased his sexual stimulation.

His general anxiety about sex interfered more and more with his ability to work, and his partner, who financed his undertakings, threatened to sever connections unless he gave more attention to his work. He fantasied homosexual relations with his partner, who represented to his unconscious the mother type on whom he could depend. He had practically achieved his basic ambition, which was to be dependent and supported. (During his college years he began to think about setting aside a sum of money in order to be able to retire at an early age.)

In all his dreams and fantasies, strong exhibitionism and tendencies to regress to pre-genital pleasures were obvious. His oral and anal pleasures were of outstanding importance, his genital activity being mostly in the service of competition with other men for a woman. The origin of his behavior was to be found in his earliest Oedipus constellation.

In the process of analysis, his genital symptom, impotence, was replaced by other physical symptoms, mostly intestinal and anal. When for a while he gave up his masturbatory and perverse activities and in his conscious attitude straight sexual desires became more prominent, he became preoccupied with bowel symptoms, chiefly constipation, for which he occasionally had to take enemas, and pruritis of the anal region of such severity that he consulted a skin specialist. All these symptoms, of course, were of a conversion hysterical nature and their aim was to strengthen the defense against becoming more potent sexually.

It took many months of hard work to make a small gain, because of his varied resistances, outstanding among which were the continually changing physical symptoms. During this period he was depressed and the memories of early loneliness were revived. He lost interest in sex and was preoccupied only with bowel activity or lack of it. He displayed a hostile attitude in the transference relationship, constantly fighting analysis and attacking the analyst. His chief complaints were that analysis had deprived him of the only type of pleasure and gratification he had had, made him lonely, and even less effective at his job.

These complaints are usual in analysis, and from the patient's viewpoint are justified. For instance, in the case of a homosexual who has made a fair adjustment, analysis may disturb the adjustment and yet not always be able to help find a more normal type of gratification. When consulted by patients with perverse tendencies to which they have made a fair adjustment, it is advisable to consider carefully whether or not analytic treatment should be instituted.

This patient frequently complained about the disturbance of his sexual activity, saying that he came to analysis because of difficulties in his work and in social life, not to have his sexual pleasure interfered with. In this negative period he made use of ample opportunities to bring up all his early prohibited and repressed desires. His childhood fears of his father especially, and also of being overheard and punished by his mother, were revived in relation to the analyst. He learned to recognize and understand all his emotional entanglements because despite his abuses and attacks on the analyst, he felt that the analyst understood the conflicts of his childhood and would not punish, criticize, or reject him for his aggressive behavior. He was convinced that he could rely on the analyst. This confidence and trust in the analyst's understanding, and the feeling that the analyst is not just a shadow, but a real person, will make effective the interpretation of resistances in negative phases.

The greatest difficulty this patient had to overcome was the acceptance of the fact that his sexuality of which he had always boasted, being especially proud of the number of women with whom he had had relations, was only a pseudo-sexuality. The feelings he described as strong sexual urges when in the company of women and even his very potent erections, were actually nothing more than an expression of his need to hide the fact that his main gratification was obtained through voyeuristic and exhibitionistic practises and fantasies. His exhibitionistic tendencies were of great importance to him. They were really an over-compensation for his castration fear. His preoccupation with the female penis fantasy was a cause of the strong voyeuristic drives. His interest in sucking the clitoris had a deeper meaning, that of making sure there was a female penis and of course also identifying the female penis with the breast. The hidden motive was to reassure himself, as if to say: "It is not true that a woman has no penis. I ascertain that she has by playing with it and sucking it, and so I do not have to fear losing my own". The voyeuristic tendencies were directed at confirming the existence of the female penis, looking for it everywhere and trying to discover it on women.

He had to practise cunnilingus and indulge in fellatio in order to function in intercourse. I induced him to give associations and try to explain his preference for these practices. In the same manner, when he indulged in exhibitionism or voyeuristic tendencies, I tried to bring forth all his ideas relating to the pleasures which he experienced in that way and why he preferred them to coitus. He was able to recognize that cunnilingus had many advantages over sexual intercourse. It carried less fear and guilt than did intercourse with its castration threat.

Oral pleasures are not forbidden to children, whereas genital activity is. Further, cunnilingus does not impregnate and there is no threat of venereal infection (so the patient näively thought). In addition, to debase himself before his partner, gratified his masochism. This practice also satisfied his infantile oral cravings and thus he avoided the adult responsibility which is involved in a normal sexual relationship.

With the other types of perverse practices and fantasies, similar dissecting is done: investigating the advantages of such practices for both partners as compared with normal sexual intercourse. The patient thus gains insight into his defenses and repressions. With this insight comes the realization that his polymorphous perverse infantile sexuality, voyeuristic and exhibitionistic tendencies, sadistic and masochistic drives, are all rooted in early fixations.

The role of early childhood sexual impressions, attachments, and fixations in the creation of neurotic difficulties is readily observable in sexual difficulties. A knowledge of early fixations is of primary importance to the cure of any kind of sexual difficulty, because fundamentally, the cure involves clearing away infantile preoccupations: voyeuristic, exhibitionistic, sadistic, or masochistic tendencies, with their concomitant masturbatory activities, all are a consequence of early fixations. They all are substitute sexual gratifications. If the paths to them are closed in the process of analysis, the sexual drive in its entirety is forced to concentrate on the genital region. The first step in the technique of accomplishing that concentration is the elimination of primary anxieties concerning genital activity. Perverse tendencies like exhibitionism or voyeurism aim at avoiding or denying fear of castration. They may also express adherence to the female penis fantasy in order to alleviate the fear of castration.

All these tendencies, i.e. preoccupation with perversions, degrees of impotence, conversion hysterical symptoms (which made the patient concentrate on his body functions instead of sexual desires), and the various symptoms which were emphasized in this special case will be encountered in varying degrees in all patients who seek treatment for sexual difficulties. The problems will always be the same, transforming passivity into aggression, concentrating all the sexual libido on the genital function by closing up all childhood avenues of gratification which hitherto served as outlets for the patient's sexuality. The patient has to be able to identify himself more with his father. The approach may differ according to the personality of the patient and the analyst. The handling of the transference situation and the interpretation of the transference and dream material may vary somewhat. However, the final result must be that the patient's sexual relationships are more pleasurable, which implies an acceptance of all aspects of adult masculine functioning.

Chapter V

SEXUAL DIFFICULTIES IN THE FEMALE [1]

The therapy of psycho-sexual difficulties in women frequently is not fully satisfactory. Psychoanalysts particularly interested in feminine psychology have noted this fact. Many have therefore concluded that they must be content if they can help the patient to adjust herself to incomplete sexual gratification and to sublimate the sexual desire by converting the penis envy (which some analysts regard as the central problem) into the wish for a child. Nevertheless we cannot accept this solution as the final aim of therapeutic endeavor; least of all, if we understand the pathogenesis of this inability to attain complete sexual gratification. To assume that one single problem is responsible for all the difficulties is to impede our progress toward a solution from the very start.

Psychoanalytic literature presents a variety of approaches to the problems of feminine psychology and sexuality. The consensus of all the investigators (whose material was gathered from many different patients) indicates that the major factors in the conflicts creating vaginal anaesthesia are: Oedipus fixation, unconscious guilt accompanying aggression towards both parents, masculinity strivings, rejection of femininity, and penis envy. Although these investi-

---

[1] The first part of this chapter contains excerpts from an article entitled "Contribution to the Problem of Vaginal Orgasm," by S. Lorand. *Int. J. Psa.*, Vol. XXII, 1939.

gators have added to the understanding of feminine psychology and helped patients to adjust better to social and sexual life, still, in the treatment of frigidity they have not always succeeded in bringing about pleasurable orgasm. An important reason for this failure, I believe, is the incomplete analysis of sensation in the vagina. Patients who complain of sexual anaesthesia or inability to reach vaginal orgasm during intercourse, can describe in detail vaginal sensations of greatly varying degree, quality, and location. If these variations are to be understood they must be thoroughly analyzed.

In the initial phase of analysis complaints of sexual anaesthesia are nearly uniform but as analysis progresses, slight yet important differences emerge. For further progress and better understanding, these slight changes in vaginal sensation must receive continuous detailed analysis. The usual complaints are: absence of any sensation in the vagina during coitus or vaginal excitement accompanied by tenseness and irritability, or extreme pain during intercourse. At times various feelings are attributed to circumscribed parts of the vagina: for instance, sensations in the upper, but none in the lower region. Or, if at first they confuse the clitoral and vaginal sensations, later in the course of analysis they learn to distinguish between clitoral, superficial vaginal, and deeper vaginal sensations. Sometimes relaxation is attained but with no other gratification. As analysis progresses these sensations may change in character as well as in location; itching and griping pulsations may occur during the analytical hour and also at other times, and may last for days and be accompanied by insatiable and even unendurable desire to feel the penis constantly within the vagina. Desire is felt as a hunger sensation of a sucking nature, with keen excitement before intercourse, but with no gratification. The vagina was called a monster, constantly hungry, by one woman who felt that before and during intercourse she was a great big mouth eating herself up because she could not attain orgasm. Coitus was always very painful to her, but the desire to have the penis in her vagina made her endure it. She could not relax from her excited state because she feared she would not be satisfied. When later she was able to achieve orgasm, it was accompanied by angry shrieking and a grasping sensation as if her vagina "reached out like an octopus". The tension just before orgasm was characterized as an "inability to let go".

The varied vaginal sensations described by patients are all of the oral type and the inability to cope with the reality of sexual functioning has its deepest roots in the earliest mother fixation. The constant hunger for affection, guidance, and dependence, the need to be 'filled up', characteristic of all these patients is mainly responsible for the failure to attain sexual gratification. In all, the equation of "Vagina=Mouth" is dominant. This problem of orality, the identification of vagina with mouth, is stressed by other authors. The importance of the little girl's attachment to her mother and its relation to the disturbance of female sexuality have been studied by Ernest Jones and others of the British group. In his latest writings

Freud again stressed the significance of the pre-history of women in the understanding of female psychology.

In that early infantile period the eating-up and filling-up tendencies predominate and are closely linked to the mother. When these patients are grown women their sexual attitude still preserves the desires, distrust, aggression, and fears persisting from the early mother attachments. In adult life they express the same aggression and fear, after frustration of the unconscious desires for the mother's body. They desire to be filled up precisely as they did in childhood, to be big, and like their mother, to have everything inside of themselves. Such wishes implied possession of the mother so as to monopolize her affection and attention. This was the basis of identification with her. (It is interesting that although this type of patient expresses a wish to be as different as possible from their mothers, curiously enough, in most cases they turn out to be very much like them.) In childhood all the body openings served the purpose of being filled up and in the adult patients the same tendency prevails. Their envy and aggression was aimed at the mother's body which contained the father's penis and the other children, all of which made her big and powerful. Childhood envy of siblings' breast-feeding and resentment at it became in adult life a source not only of guilt but also of fear that their own bodies would be destroyed in their eating, coitus, menstruation, pregnancy, and childbirth. Ernest Jones has shown that there is more femininity in the young girl than analysts gener ally recognize, and has stressed the need for analysis of her earliest period of attachment to her mother. Melanie Klein, and others too, have pointed out the consequences of this most significant period. I feel strongly that the success of therapy of neurotic difficulties in women depends on the solution of this decisive infantile attachment. Especially is this so when the fears and aggressions resulting from early frustration by the mother are carried over to the field of adult sexual function. As a result, the entire sexual life of these patients is disrupted. Their flight from sexual pleasures is caused by fear of repeated frustrations as in the early mother attachment. There is fear of losing the penis before achieving orgasm, that coitus will end and they will be compelled to surrender the male organ. This is not, as some analysts think, the same as the desire to have a penis, the wish to be a boy: it is fear of losing the father's penis which they wanted to acquire but had to renounce. This may be amplified to mean: giving up something they wanted in childhood, as they wanted their mother's body and her love. In this instance the word *love* includes varied objects and emotions: the mother (for affection and dependence); the other children (as rivals and enviable objects); the penis, breast, and food (things desirable to have, to acquire, and not relinquish); all these are included under the general heading of love. When the orgasm is inhibited, it is because of fear of losing this love (breast, penis, affection, and so forth), and of being left alone, apart, and empty.

Some analysts have conjectured that vaginal sensations are present before as well as after puberty, but that they are due to vaginal play. However, even without definite memory of vaginal masturbation, the presence of such sensations in early years can be substantiated from the age of three upwards. Some patients have given definite evidence of knowledge about the vagina and its functioning at the early age of three. Though this knowledge later became confused, it was never completely repressed or denied. We may assume the presence of an early vaginal phase in the little girl, for the assumption that the little girl does not recognize the existence of the vagina is not borne out by facts; nor is it definitely established that lack of a penis always troubles her, or that possessing one would satisfy her. Some patients had thought about having a penis but never actually desired to own one as an appendage outside the body. Certainly they admitted wishing for one, but for an internal one. One patient expressed her childhood desire in this manner: at the age of six she pulled her little brother on top of her, with the wish to put his penis inside her vagina, but then realized that his penis was too small, for she knew it was a big one she wanted.

It should be noted here that the attitude typical of such patients was that of wanting to acquire something and then tenaciously holding on to it. Especially was this attitude characteristic of their sexuality. The escape from sexual pleasure (exemplified by their frigidity) was an expression of the fear of losing something they had already acquired: possibly their pride and adjustment without the pleasure of coitus. Fearing dependence upon a man's penis for their sexual pleasure, they indulged instead in clitoral masturbation. In coitus, when they had already experienced all the preliminary pleasure sensations, their excitement (even to the point of climax), the fear of coming to orgasm, their "not letting go", all reproduced the early pattern of purely oral dependence and oral receptiveness which ended in frustration. It was the repetition of that pattern that they feared.

One patient who suffered from severe anorexia, in addition to many other neurotic and character difficulties, had the symptom of vomiting, associated with the fantasy that she had swallowed her father's penis. In her fantasy it lingered inside her. She described the process as a circular one: swallowing, going into her body, coming out at the bottom, again going up to her mouth, swallowing, etc. In the process of analysis she became afraid to relax on the couch because of sexual feelings in her vagina and fear that the analyst, who was a woman, might insert something into her vagina. The whole fantasy and its resultant symptom meant: a desire to swallow her father's penis, (intercourse with him,) becoming pregnant (having it in her stomach), and then finally childbirth (vomiting it out). To incorporate the penis, first by the mouth, later by the vagina, is, as Jones pointed out, the realization of the little girl's primary wish for the penis. Naturally her dependence on her mother and her simultaneous aggressive defiance towards her, were the driving forces behind her neurotic symptoms. She actually and consciously employed vomiting to express hostility to her mother.

In another patient this orality was expressed in

her vaginal aims, and was unmistakable in her manner of masturbation and fantasy. She used to masturbate by withholding her urine. The pleasurable sensations increased in proportion to the fantasied filling up of the bladder. It was a cavity which she in fantasy tried to fill up from an outside source. Simultaneously in this fantasy a man whom she liked very much was forcibly trying to impregnate her. Although she protested, the protest itself was a source of pleasure. These sensations which she would provoke by fantasy were experienced high up in the vagina. She also experienced a remarkable series of sensations in her mouth and teeth especially when speaking. At times she awoke at night with pains in her teeth which a dentist could not explain. As analysis advanced she resented the gradual awakening of sensitivity in the vagina. As she put it: when she came to analysis, she had no vagina at all, she was not aware of it. Now she was all vagina. Constantly excited, preoccupied with sexual fantasies, tortured mentally by pulsation in her vagina, she felt she was losing herself and being destroyed with desire. She wished for perpetual intercourse. Incidentally she was notorious for a prodigious appetite and continual eating. In the advanced stages of her analysis she had pleasurable feelings in coitus but stopped short of orgasm for she felt rising hatred towards her partner since she feared he might take away his penis and give it to another woman. For this reason she was preoccupied throughout intercourse with the thought that something must not happen. She also resented orgasm because she wanted continued coitus.

These attitudes obviously paralleled her feelings toward her mother whom she resented for taking the breast away from her to give it to siblings. The fear that something terrible might follow intercourse was connected with her childhood fantasies of destruction of the mother's body because of repeated pregnancies. Worth noting is the fact that this patient had no memory of her mother as pregnant or nursing, although she was old enough to remember, and could recall seeing in that same period other pregnant women and other women breast-feeding their babies in the street.

The same early tie to the mother's breast, the same feminine passive accepting attitude, and strong feminine identification were exhibited by another patient. She had a vivid recollection of vaginal sensations occurring between the ages of five and six. At that time she had contracted a vaginal infection from another girl and had to use a douche. Following that period she practised vaginal masturbation. She had been sleeping in the same room with her parents for years and the noises she heard of parental intercourse excited her and induced masturbation. In marriage during coitus she displayed violent body movements, screamed and bit her husband (all this developed in the course of analysis) but she could not reach orgasm because of the constant fear that her husband would ejaculate too soon. By working through her dreams, associations, and emotions, interesting and important material emerged revealing a deep attachment to her mother and shocking childhood experiences at her hands. Another patient recalled that she knew all the facts of childbirth at the age of about five or six. At that time when a sibling was born she heard her mother instruct someone to hide the bloody sheets from the patient's observation. Thus she came to connect childbirth with bleeding and injury to the region of the vagina.

Clinical observation shows us that the problem of feminine sexual anaesthesia is much more complicated than is generally understood. Although analysts have long attempted to formulate the causes of these difficulties, their therapeutic results have not kept pace with their theoretic formulations. The period Freud calls "dim and shadowy", the pre-Oedipal phase of the little girl, is the period in which we must seek the basic cause for the sexual difficulty. We find that all women with such difficulties make their mothers responsible for their own lack of an affectionate disposition. In the analytical process they express it thus: when they develop vaginal sensations and the desire for intercourse, they accuse the analyst of throwing them back upon other men, just as in childhood the mother forced them to look to the father for affection. Out of spite and resentment they refuse to enjoy coitus. They look upon a mother as a dangerous person, injurious to everyone. Another important factor in the frigid reaction is the patients' idea that the mother's sexual life with the father cannot be pleasurable. This belief is caused by the feeling that their own hostility to mother may have interfered with her sexual pleasure. In fantasy they actually did try to hinder her enjoyment. Their flight from femininity is a reaction to this aggression and consequent fear of the mother. They cannot identify themselves and find pleasure in vaginal sensation and intercourse. Only when they accept the idea in analysis that their mother may have enjoyed this relationship can they permit themselves to experience pleasurable sensation. Another reason for their flight from femininity is the feeling of inferiority, which is not only an expression of penis envy but in a much deeper sense involves a comparison of mother and child. They resent having to depend on the penis for gratification and on the possessor of the penis for food and support. It recalls painfully their oral dependence in childhood and its many frustrations. The child feels weak and small compared to the mother, and the penis envy refers to the father's penis (affection) of which the mother was the sole recipient.

From the therapeutic results and the material presented by many patients in long analyses one comes to the conclusion that vaginal sensations are primary and that infantile masturbation cannot be described as exclusively clitoral or labial. It involves clitoris, labia, and vagina. The theory that the clitoral sensations are primary and have to be transferred to the vagina cannot be substantiated. In analysis the clitoral sensations lose their importance because the woman re-discovers and re-learns early infantile sensations in the vagina which were repressed, forgotten, and could not be enjoyed. The vagina can now be accepted and does not have to be denied because it is "an evil and dangerous organ like the mouth which wants to devour everything and everybody", as Ernest Jones has pointed out.

In analysis it will always be found that the deep emotional difficulties and unconscious mechanisms at the base of female sexual disturbances are bound up with their strong early oral fixation, remnants of which are directly apparent in their behavior and character. During therapy, these patients also must go through emotional difficulties, feel them and understand them. They have to learn to accept their fantasies, unconscious attitudes, and impulses and will develop the ability to handle their difficulties.

The following case shows the powerful opposing forces in the woman's unconscious and the variety of difficulties which inhibit vaginal orgasm and normal sexual functioning. The manner in which her sexual difficulties were changed, then reduced, and finally eliminated gave a clear picture of the developmental history of her difficulties.

This patient was in her late twenties when she came for treatment. She complained of severe anxiety spells and during the first interview she herself connected her anxiety with her confusion about and fear of sex. Before coming to me, she had been in treatment with two other colleagues and in both instances had succeeded in bringing about the disruption of the analysis through her temper-tantrum-like spells and aggressive attitude.

She came of a well-to-do family. Of her father, who died when she was about five, she did not remember much. Because of her mother's behavior, the picture she presented of her childhood, puberty, and adolescence, to the age of sixteen was colored with hate and defiance and full of mental anguish. At the age of sixteen she broke away from home and soon afterwards established herself in a manner that she considered independent although she still depended on money from home. She found a male friend and from then on her life was a series of emotional disturbances which she always attributed to her restless driving for men.

Her first so-called love affair she planned in advance and kept up the relationship for about a year. The other affairs were mainly "pick-ups", and she managed to be picked up by all classes of men. Experiences with different men did not bring real differences in her sexual pleasure with them. It was obvious that she never was completely satisfied and sexual intercourse to her was a narcissistic activity, bolstering her ego; it was as if she were collecting male genitals as trophies.

In the analysis for a long time she displayed negativistic tendencies. Aggression and stubbornness were the outstanding characteristics. Her voice and her carriage expressed aggression. She spoke with vehemence; her speech consisted of choppy, short, emphatic sentences. The object of her sexual relationships was to hurt the man. In analysis it became evident that her going from one man to the other was a means of seeking revenge against father and mother. The mother's puritanical attitude, education, and constant scolding and warning from childhood on up through adolescence, made the patient enraged and defiant. In her promiscuous sexual relationships she carried over this disobedience. Also she wanted revenge against the father for having left the family. (He had died shortly after having effected a separation from his wife.) In all her memories of him up to the age of five, he was tender and loving, and she remembered being cared for by him. It was the deep longing for a father, for a man, that drove her to seek men and to run from one man to another. There was also a strong identification with the male, that had its root in her relationship with the father and brother. She expressed it in analysis by saying that she felt as if she had been robbed by her brothers. She should have been the man because her brothers had builds and characters more feminine than hers and she could have been a much better man than ony one of them, was how she felt about it. She really believed that her mother was responsible for making the brothers males. However, in her unconscious she never gave up the strong desire to be a man and her many affairs served the additional purpose of gratifying her desire to always have a penis inside her. She achieved most gratification by cunnilingus and fellatio. On closer examination these modes of gratification showed various components. Fellatio satisfied her masculine tendencies and her desire to have the man dependent upon her. Cunnilingus served her desire to humiliate him. In addition these practices eliminated her fear of bodily destruction from sexual activity, her fear of infection, and most important of all, the involvement which sexual intercourse meant to her in early childhood, i.e., taking father away from mother, and pregnancy by father. From childhood on she thought many times about her father's probably unsatisfactory love life with her mother and felt that he left home because of mother. She wished he were alive so she could make up to him all his unhappiness with mother. In her unconscious all men represented her father. In her fantasies the penis was always in an erect state. Her indulging in fellatio and the pleasure she derived from it were due mainly to infantile oral cravings, the penis equalling breast and she the sucking baby.

She was troubled most by her anxiety spells, which at the deepest level, were connected with her mother's constant intimidation of her when a little girl. The mother's attitude succeeded in making her shy, morose, and given to brooding when she was still a child. She felt that her mother was responsible for her father's abandonment of them, and adding that to her other experiences, she was convinced that her mother was a dangerous woman who dominated everybody and rejected her and father. She learned, also when very young, that her mother was not to be trusted, nor indeed a father who could abandon his child. Finally she came to feel that she could depend on no one and this distrust permeated her sexual life as well, causing her to resent the fact that she had to depend on a man for gratification. Though in her sexual relationships she became stimulated she did not reach an orgasm, because of her wish to maintain her independence. Having an orgasm meant, to her, losing her head, being reduced to helplessness, therefore she could not give in to her desire for sexual gratification. Early in life she determined never to show weakness, never to be at the mercy of any person, never to become dependent because that would end in frustration. Thus her whole life became a struggle between her feminine dependence and her unconscious masculine drives. Her womanly qualities served as a mask behind which she was constantly tortured with the conflicts of masculinity. She could not trust any man's affection for her. At the same time she felt unworthy of love and believed that she herself was responsible for all her troubles. However, she had conflicts about these sentiments also as was shown in her complaints of having been pushed in the background, always having been scolded by mother, and of living in constant dread of punishment. She realized that her relationships with men were an expression of defiance against her upbringing and home in general. It took her a long time to see that although she never forgave her parents and siblings for treating her as she claimed they did, there were also present strong feelings of need of their love.

It may seem paradoxical to speak of a castration complex in females. In this patient it can more readily be understood since she tried in every way to be masculine. Moreover, her jealousy and fear of men caused her to want to deprive them of their masculinity. The sexual contacts with men meant reassurance to her, gratification of her need for self-esteem. She had fantasies of women commanding men to work and fantasies of men being forced to copulate with many women in succession. Their difficulties, in both fantasies, were a source of pleasure to her. Another daydream was of a rubbish cart being pushed by a streetcleaner whom she caught, cut up, and threw into the cart.

At times she was very much concerned about the man who seemed to have formed an attachment to her. She felt sorry for him and tried to prevent him from becoming strongly attached. However, this solicitude covered her own aggression and self-defense. She really wanted to harm him, to make him dependent upon her, and then to abandon him as she had been abandoned in childhood by her father. On the other hand, she feared that she might become attached to and dependent upon him.

Her castration complex really referred to her enormous penis envy. It made her, as she expressed it, the kind of person who definitely would have become a prostitute. She would have loved to pick up her men from the street, but her education and upbringing prevented her from going all the way. She felt at times when having such urges, that her vagina was on fire and that sexual activity did not reduce this sensation. It was like having a devil inside her, she said. On those occasions she obtained relief by masturbating while having the fantasy of being whipped. During the period of her strong transference relationship, she began to experience vaginal sensations which she had never known before. It was during this period that she was able to let down her guard completely and talk about her rich and colorful sexual fantasies. In the course of the discussions in the analytical hour, she felt sensations which she described as pulsating, exciting, and irritating at the same time. When away from the office, she felt sensations of insatiable desire in her vagina and was afraid to come to analysis. She dreaded to lie down on the couch because of vaginal sensations and it embarrassed her acutely to report that she felt a discharge. When at home, she masturbated and had many orgasms in succession. Her fantasies were associated with the analyst; wanting to be loved by him, to have his finger in her vagina which she felt was wide open like a hungry, waiting mouth. Then she produced angry violent fantasies in the analytical session, of throwing and nailing penises and testicles on the wall. When vaginal sensations and craving for affection became forceful, she acted aggressively in her sexual relationship, but her conception of coitus was an extremely masochistic one. She had cherished masochistic fantasies in which she indulged from the time she began to have sex relationships. One was centered around a fat ugly man who was violent and forced her to have intercourse in all kinds of positions. In this fantasy fellatio also entered; she pretended that he was forcing her to swallow his penis which was nearly choking her. The fantasy of a constantly erect penis also carried the threat of a powerful man and it was an expression of her secret desire to have such a penis herself, a desire she tried to realize by constantly changing partners and accumulating innumerable penises. The fat, ugly man was unmasked in analysis and proved to be the dentist who took care of her teeth when she was between six and seven years of age, and of whom she was mortally afraid. The figure also represented her father whom she had to make into a powerful ugly person in accordance with her childhood fantasies that sexual intercourse was a sadistic, cruel act, forced upon the woman. To be tortured in sex also served her need to expiate the guilt of her Œdipus desires. If she suffered she could indulge in the forbidden sexual act.

Another fantasy of much earlier origin with which she frequently masturbated, was of being whipped by nuns. She is discovered wetting her panties, they are slowly pulled off her, she is gradually exposed which excites her very much, then she is whipped. To convert the strong masochism which these two fantasies carried, apart from their sexual aspect, was a tedious and difficult process. Being whipped by nuns in connection with wetting herself was a later construction. Originally the fantasy was "I am being beaten by father," which meant the reverse: being loved by father and given his attention. In the transference relationship this fantasy constantly reappeared with reference to the analyst. It was also directly related to the fantasy of the ugly man. The original fantasy of being whipped meant being sexually attacked by father; it was the early feminine Œdipus attitude. In analysis she brought forth the recollection that originally she used to fantasy that nuns were being whipped by men. This referred definitely to her early conception of intercourse between her parents (father torturing mother and forcing it upon her). Being whipped by nuns referred to mother, who from the time the patient was five, was the strong, punishing parent.

As far back as she could remember, the "wet panties" constantly preoccupied mother, who was always warning her and the other children, always questioning and sending them to the bathroom before going for a walk. As late as the age of ten her mother used to feel her pants to see whether they were dry. This made her furious, but also carried the feeling of pleasure because the attention meant fondling to her. However, she felt that she had been a fool to be so perfect a child, never to have wet the bed, because in spite of it, mother did not love her. This feeling aggravated her hatred of her mother and gave an added impetus to sexual fantasies about father. The masochistic fantasies thus took care of the guilt arising from her feelings toward parents.

What she termed her "dangerous sexual appetite" slowly turned into an ever increasing childish need for dependence and craving for love in the transference relationship. The extreme sadistic fantasies, the aggressiveness which in analysis produced fantasies like cooking carrots, which turn into penises, or chopping off penises and throwing them into an ashcan, or splitting the analyst in half, changed into the type of fantasies like: a big head is looking at her genital, she is standing with her tiny feet on the analyst's lap, her arms around his neck (being a small baby), or, a fantasy of having intercourse with the analyst, during which he encourages her, saying it is right to have it.

In this stage of her treatment, analysis gave her conscious gratification (partly erotic), which she desired to retain. She needed the gratification which is afforded by the opportunity of talking and being listened to, which she did not have during childhood.

Only the boys had received that attention at home and they had managed the mother much better than she had. Her anxiety in the analytical situation was still maintained and her symptoms pointed to ambivalence towards the analyst. Her wish to depend and fear of the consequences were always uppermost in her mind. Basically she wanted to be feminine, to have a masculine man, not to conquer but to be conquered. At times she felt that she had to have a relationship with a man right then and there, in order to feel secure and to know that she could have coitus if she so desired. This attitude referred to her belief in the elusive quality of men, including the analyst, and went back to her early abandonment by father. It accounted for her wanting to handle sex in her own way which would eliminate fear of dependence and ultimate frustration. However, her desire for dependence came more and more to the fore and her acceptance of this fundamental wish, ceasing to fight against it and permitting it to become a part of her, was slowly accomplished.

Her previous unconscious attitude toward intercourse, which had prevailed during the years before and in the early phase of analysis, can be summed up as follows: "I acquired independence from my mother. I want independence from men. I don't want to be dependent upon anybody for gratification". At that time she referred to herself as "impotent"; she could not bring herself to say "frigid".

When she had reached the stage where she derived conscious gratification from analysis, her attitude was modified to: "Struggle against dependence for gratification upon man. Intercourse is painful. I cannot love because it will be used against me and will expose me to the whim of the person to whom I confess love".

This later attitude also changed gradually as a result of the vicissitudes of her emotional involvements in the transference relationship.

All her difficulties stemmed from the original strong oral attachment to the mother and afterwards to the father. The original desire to take in everything and to become as strong as the mother through the mother's feeding and nursing, was transferred to the father and to his penis from which one might develop a large stomach, become big. But this much coveted food had poisonous qualities as well for her. Semen equalled food. This food might harm one in the same way that the mother was made ill during pregnancy. Just as food might be desired but injurious (in line with the mother's admonitions about over-eating, eating candy, finger-sucking) so, too, sexual intercourse might be desired but might prove harmful. The aggression and fear which originated in those early years, because of frustration of oral cravings, were directly responsible for her inability to love, which in turn affected her entire sexual life. The idea of having her own penis, which appeared in dreams related to striving for independence from both men and women, was her attempt to renounce love. This was the result of having to accept the fact that father and mother belonged to each other and she, being excluded, had to give up both father and mother (breast and penis) at a very early period. Her penis envy and penis wish developed later. The original wish, which came back in full strength during the period of her constant sexual excitement, was to have the penis inside, continually, permanently, never having to relinquish it. In all its ramifications, it proved to be the original strong oral craving. It created hostility and guilt which had to be expiated by her intense masochism. She wished to experience all the disappointments of childhood in order to fulfill her masochistic, self-punishing needs. She would impatiently await coming to treatment, but once there would act panicky, complain of difficulty in breathing, implore help and assurance of love. She would experience genital sensations, and want the analyst's love but would reject all sympathy and reassurance.

The Œdipus conflict became a reality to her through her changing feelings in analysis and the relationship with and sexual desire for the analyst. She understood then, that the violence which she felt all through her lifetime was connected with the anxiety spells and referred to earliest strong desires for affection by both parents. These feelings were colored with hostility directed mainly towards the mother for depriving her of the father. This aggression was one of the main barriers to her enjoyment of sex life. Her flight from femininity was also a reaction against her mother; since she was unable to identify with her, she could not accept femininity, therefore abnormal feelings ruled her whole sex life.

During the reactivation of the Œdipus period, she had the following dream:

"I am telling mother how horrible she was to me. Then the analyst invites me to go into his car and

I accept just to be polite, though I would prefer to go on my own bicycle."

The meaning of the dream was quite obvious, but she also expressed, in the associations to it, the desire to like people, not to hate them. "I pretended for years to be hard-boiled. I had to protect myself from the stupidity of people. Now I have a marvelous contact with them and I want to show myself as I really am. I think it came about because you (the analyst) did not lie to me. All former doctors cheated me. One of my former doctors promised not to talk about me to the analyst who had sent me to him, but he did. The doctor before that one did not believe the story of how the first analyst dismissed me." It was true, to some extent, that her confidence in the analyst and her feeling that he was honest, gave her a chance to identify with him, since he represented a different type of mother than her own was, and to believe that there are straightforward people in the world.

During the same period she had another dream which indicated the progress of her treatment: "Great amounts of dirt came out of me." Her associations brought out her fear of venereal disease, pregnancy, abortion, and the like, and she added the following remark: "I am beginning to feel sensuous, this time in my body, not in my head. It is so precious that I am afraid it may disappear." Quite obviously there was a conflict between the newly acquired desires and the old ideas and distrust of men. However, her concept of sex and men had changed considerably by this time. The man was no longer an appendix to a penis. Now she wanted the man close; she desired to be loved by him and to have sexual gratification through his penis. She no longer resented dependence on the penis for gratification nor did she resent dependence on a man for food and support.

During her lengthy analysis, it was possible to differentiate specific periods according to the symptoms which prevailed most strongly in the various stages. Her complaints were all intensified by the transference situation.   Her attitudes towards vaginal sensations were of special significance because through their slow and gradual change from pain to toleration and from then on through the different degrees of pleasurable sensation to the point where she was able to reach the peak of excitement (still without orgasm, however), through this process, her complex neurosis became comprehensible to her.   Once she became stronger, she could accept the impulses with all the force behind them and learn to use them in a healthy manner. Thus the ultimate goal of her treatment, which is related to all cases of feminine sexual anesthesia, was accomplished to a great extent: without much rebellion to accept femininity, and that implies accepting all the pain and fear which feminine sexual functions like menstruation or pregnancy, may cause.

The strong oral erotic tendencies which enter into the character structure in cases with sexual difficulties make the technique of therapy rather complicated. The insatiable sexual hunger of these women is an unconscious expression of their early childhood hunger for love.   In the cases cited their distrust which appeared in the transference relationship in the form of hostility, was a reaction to the frustrated sexual desires for the analyst. This desire really meant the wish to be accepted and approved of just as in early childhood the sexual desires for father carried the wish for approval. The Œdipus situation is the core of the problem just as in male sexual difficulties, but in female sexual disturbances pre-Œdipal desires and disappointments further complicate the situation. Many suggestions had to be given to the patient in the course of analysis, especially in regard to controlling her tendencies to act out her feelings. When sexually excited and at the same time frustrated in the analytical situation, her former promiscuous tendencies returned in full force. She was ready to enter into a sexual affair with any man. I tried to control her impulsiveness by constant interpretation of her desires and also by explaining that guilt feelings would follow such behavior. The same methods were used to check masturbation. At a certain stage of her analysis she was inclined to act out in her social relationships her general feeling of hostility. This was interfered with by re-directing those feelings to the analytical situation. Through ventilating both positive and negative feelings she slowly learned to be less afraid of "letting go", a fear which was largely responsible for her frigidity. She could not relax and have an orgasm because that would have meant being unconscious for a second, losing control. That loss of control she could not permit, even for a moment because of her fear of what she might do. She really feared the breaking through of her hostility against men and her desire to do violence to them. In the act of coitus, the refusal to "let go" also meant not letting go of the male genital. As long as she felt the penis, her unconscious masculine desire to possess a phallus was gratified and all her problems of submission, masochism, inferiority to men, were thus temporarily solved. Her desire for perpetual intercourse was also due to strong penis envy and masculine identification, both of which are clearly expressed in the following dream:

"A girl friend takes me to her room to show me her paintings. In her room she opens her blouse. Instead of two breasts, she has one big thing in the middle. It is reddish, like the penis of a horse. She says that she was operated on and this is the result. I was disgusted with the sight, then I had it on my body, held it in my hand and was not disgusted any more."

The meaning of the dream is obvious. Her associations to it again expressed her confusion about the meaning of her masculine drives.

Not reaching an orgasm was, to her, another way of castrating the man. Also, by not reacting, she reassured herself of her own power and independence, i.e., not allowing him to produce a change in her, while she could manipulate him according to her will, first causing him to be passionate and have an erection, then taking his erection away and leaving him weak.

Therapy in such an extreme case is a very tedious, lengthy process. The phase of analysis, during which most of the adjustment on the part of the patient takes place, can be a very long drawn out period. In this phase, the patient gradually recognizes that the transference desires cannot be gratified by the analyst and then slowly tries to manage without the analyst. However, again and again old transference wishes flare up and the patient must experience frustration anew. In this manner the ego attitude is slowly and gradually strengthened and leads to a final relinquishing of desires concerning the therapist.

In the case cited, various phases were clearly differentiated and the transitions from one to the other readily apparent during the lengthy therapeutic process. The patient started out with no vaginal orgasm, though she was able to reach an orgasm through clitoral stimulation by her male partner. As treatment progressed she achieved an orgasm through vaginal masturbation accompanied by fantasies of being beaten and tortured by the man. Later on she reached orgasm with masturbation fantasies about the analyst (i.e., that his finger was in her vagina), no longer having fantasies of being beaten.

All during this period she also had sexual intercourse, but only the friction on the clitoris, either by hand or penis accompanied by her fantasies, led to orgasm. Then came a period of lasting for months when intercourse was rendered impossible by vaginal cramps. Masturbation or the penetration of her partner's finger was painful, and although it gave her some slight sexual excitement it also produced anxiety. During this period she openly rebelled against men, but at the same time she had the desire to appear more and more feminine, the desire to be supported by a man and to be dependent on him. After working through that phase, there was a renewal of erotic fantasies, this time about the type of man in her social stratum, (in actual affairs she had always chosen someone below her social group), and she also contemplated pregnancy.

This period marked a renewed interest in sexual intercourse; she spoke about relearning to enjoy it, and at the same time rejected fellatio and was disgusted by cunnilingus.

Chapter VI

COMPULSION NEUROSIS

The conglomeration of bizarre and contradictory symptoms and behavior that are found in compulsion neuroses presents an extremely difficult problem for the therapist. As a result of their ever present ambivalence, the powerful antagonism between love and hate, these patients wish to be dependent while feeling rebellious, exhibit a neat and clean appearance but are secretly impelled to dirtiness, have heterosexual ambitions which are countered by homosexual regressions, strong destructive tendencies accompanied by equally strong feelings of guilt. They desire to be good and bad at the same time.

Compulsion neurotics try to eliminate or relieve with magic thoughts and actions the discomfort (at times amounting to torture) caused by the antagonistic strivings. Instead of affording relief, however, these rituals further complicate their obsessive problems.

Freud's analysis of compulsion neurosis has provided us with a basic understanding of it and a formulation of its psychodynamics. To his original interpretation much has been added by more recent contributors. The studies of Abraham and Jones concerning the conflicts of the compulsion neurotic and the connection between obsessional conflicts and anal regression have enlarged the theory, aided in classification, and made the symptom complex of this neurosis more comprehensible. Ferenczi's description of

117

the early super-ego formation and its connection with the pregenital phase of development was a further important contribution.

The usual complaint of the analyst is that the patient's symptoms and his carrying them to absurdity make the treatment tedious and unproductive. There is a good deal that at first seems obscure and puzzling in the symptom complex but with proper handling therapy can be successful. The prognosis for therapeutic success depends on various factors, among which the age of the patient is of paramount importance. The younger the patient, the better the prognosis, but older people can also be benefited to a very marked degree. In the symptom manifestation, various contradictory impulses find expression; the constant shifts and changes in the feelings of the patient make it difficult for the analyst to maintain empathy with the patient's moods. Many therapists lose patience and become discouraged; hence the literature on the subject reflects varying opinions as to treatment and possible results.

The tendency to regress to the anal stage of development (which immediately precedes the fully developed Œdipus phase) results in the strong ambivalence and narcissistic involvement characteristic of the compulsion neuroses. But the pregenital drives that have such an important role in the creation of the patient's neurosis do not completely achieve their goal of forcing the patient to regress to the anal phase. Strong Œdipal tendencies and genital drives can be detected in the symptomatology. The partial regression to the anal-sadistic, pre-Œdipal period carries with it strong drives belonging to the Œdipal phase.

This overlapping creates an additional difficult problem in the therapeutic process. A steady battle rages between the masculine tendencies (belonging to the genital phase) and the passive, feminine ones (which characterize the anal).

The symptom complex of the compulsion neuroses is the result of a compromise between instinctual drives and superego commands and prohibitions. At times the outstanding symptom clearly expresses the compelling force of the superego. Sometimes the compulsion represents a defense against the threat of the breaking through of instinctual drives.

Fantastic and grotesque as the obsessions and compulsions may appear, they can be understood if examined in the light of the patient's developmental history. But the relationship between symptoms and history is very difficult to uncover, and to accomplish it is sometimes a very tedious and prolonged task. The history always reveals that the instinctual tendencies were forced to expression in the particular form in which the compulsive neurotic displays them. Analysis also discloses the important role of the superego in the early period of development and will show that the obsessions are centered around the father. Indulgence and pampering during the oral and anal period of development result in grave interference with development into a normal Œdipus stage with strong genital aims. There is constant vacillation and indecision in the compulsion neuroses in regard to growing up or remaining a child: realizing genital tendencies or regressing to anal drives. The conflict ends in a compromise of partial regression to the anal-sadistic level, attempting thus to maintain some genital aims while clinging at the same time to passive anal tendencies. Further complications arise from this compromise because implicit in the genital aims is the danger of castration. In order to eliminate the fear of castration, a passive line of development is followed and homosexual, self-castrating tendencies are utilized by the patient.

The history of the compulsive neurotic will also show that in the anal phase of development the parents were actually more tolerant and attentive, permitted and encouraged more dependence than is considered normal. When the genital phase was reached, prohibitions and demands for adjustments and independence were suddenly imposed upon the child who met them with strong rebellion and aggression. As a result, powerful repression had to be employed by the child to prevent open defiance which would have caused him to be punished. Generally the last phase in the developmental history of the child in which strong dependence is present and even encouraged, is the anal phase. Because he clings to the anal-erotic phase of development, the compulsion · neurotic expects dependence and reassurance and demands it more vigorously.

The severe self-punishing tendencies which so strongly interfere with the therapeutic process are a result of repressed aggression. It becomes evident in analysis that the anal activities and functions are charged with erotic feelings and, to a certain degree, carry genital aims. The superego, which is intolerant of genital desires, punishes anal activities because they satisfy sexual feelings. Experience has repeatedly shown how strongly colored with anal tendencies the sexual life of the compulsive neurotic is: for instance, how strongly sadistic the act of intercourse is to him (amounting to an expression of the wish to get rid of dirty excretions [sexual secretion], soiling the partner).

The patient's constant struggle is between his compulsive drives and self-condemnation for giving in to them. The elaborate rituals and complicated ceremonies for security from the tendencies to rebel consume a large portion of his energies and seriously interfere with his functioning and activities. True, the protective measures become stronger in this way and the patient feels safe from the breaking through of rebellion; but at the same time the rejected, repressed impulses also become stronger. Basically all defense mechanisms are used against the emergence of desires and impulses connected with the Œdipus relationship.

The Œdipus desires, which contain genital involvement, are fraught with danger for the ego. Therefore, regression to the anal phase of development is continually attempted. Feelings of rivalry and aggression, and desires to destroy the severe superego exist side by side with their opposites: desire for protection, guidance, love, reparation by the parents, who even when thought of as frustrating, demanding persons, are *at the same time the objects of love*. The interaction of these contradictory strivings results in symptom formation.

The outstanding defense mechanisms of which the compulsive neurotic makes use are:

(1) *Isolation* of the conscious (thinking) from the unconscious (magical) part of the personality. The patient separates his feelings from the symptom, hiding its latent meaning because he dares not admit to having the feeling that the symptom conceals. Thus, because of a strong sense of guilt, his actions are disconnected from their source.

(2) *Reaction formation,* by means of which the patient covers up instinctual drives with a display of an opposite tendency. For example, he may hide rebellion and defiance under a cloak of extreme obedience, or be scrupulously clean and neat while secretly wishing to be dirty.

(3) *Undoing* unconscious drives by means of magic thoughts or gestures. This defense mechanism is always at work in the compulsion neurotic. The undoing mechanism is also applied to the passage of time. One patient (whose treatment is described further on in this chapter) confused appointments and made telephone calls late at night, trying to force his environment to be at his service irrespective of time. One might have expected him to be obsessional regarding the analytic hour, but on the contrary, he was punctual at times, sometimes late, and sometimes early. His punctuality or lack of it always had a specific, unconscious object. This patient's attitude toward the passage of time was carried over into his work habits. He would play the radio or do cross-word puzzles until midnight, then work from midnight until three or four in the morning and sleep nearly the whole day. In childhood he used to play in bed after being told to go to sleep and his father had to

punish him to make him try to sleep. He would go to the toilet when the other members of the family sat down to dinner, so that he had to be called to the table. He purposely stayed in the bathroom until he had been called many times.

He expressed his obsession regarding time by saying: "I don't want time to pass". That of course referred to his feeling of rebellion in childhood and adolescence when his parents, especially his father, wanted him to do things the moment he was asked. At the deepest level it referred to mother, oral pleasures and frustrations, sister's breast feeding when he was nearly two years old, and his rage against her (at birth he wanted to poke her eyes out) for having mother's breast. The passing of time meant growing up, something he tried to avoid by every means within his control. If he could stop time, he could always remain a child.

Still another defense against superego demands which is found in compulsion neuroses was described by Alexander as an attempt on the part of the patient to corrupt the superego. He pretends to be humble, obedient, even willing to suffer, thus expiating the guilt before sinning so that he may feel free to indulge. This type of resistance can be carried to a point where the patient is carefully obedient and overdoes all that is asked of him, just as he outwardly obeyed educational rules readily in childhood. This mode of behavior in response to analytic suggestions can succeed in making analysis appear absurd and ridiculous.

If the patient succeeds in making analysis appear nonsensical, he utilizes the situation to prove that the analyst (superego) is in the wrong; then he can feel justified in his aggression; he may even succeed in feeling equal or superior to the analyst. Under those circumstances, he feels free to indulge in gratifications which were hitherto prohibited by his superego. When confronted with these varied defenses, all of which are of a childish and primitive nature, treatment at times appears to be an impossibility.

The following case history is intended to illustrate the therapeutic process in compulsion neuroses: The patient was in his early twenties when he sought treatment but his history revealed that he had had obsessions and compulsions between the ages of nine and twelve. He was an only boy; his sister was born when he was twenty months old. He insisted in analysis that he remembered wanting to stick his finger in her eyes when she was an infant.

Around the age of nine or ten he continually asked questions of his parents when sitting at the dinner table. The habit so irritated them that he was often severely punished. He repeatedly bid good night to his parents whose bedroom door was left open at his insistence. He ceremoniously reiterated "good night" until his father silenced him, usually by shouting at him. During the same period he felt compelled to make sure that the electric light in his bathroom was turned off. The bathroom door had to be left ajar so that he could look again from his bedroom to ascertain that the light was off. He always had to look twice to be convinced, and he connected the looking twice with having two eyes. With both eyes he had to be sure that the light was out. When he had convinced himself that he saw with both eyes, he felt reassured that he was not blind. Around this time he also was impelled to touch his classmates' (boys) noses and also the nose of his governess. At about twelve he became aware of feelings of sexual excitement and had frequent erections. He questioned his father about them and the father seized the opportunity to warn him against masturbation.

These obsessions gradually disappeared but by the time he was in his early twenties (when he came for analysis) they had reappeared, and in addition he complained of a number of obsessive phobias and work inhibitions which he feared would cause him to lose his job. Outstanding among his many symptoms were obsessions concerning the toilet. He first had to make certain that the toilet was flushed and after that he had to be sure that the water stopped running. After washing his hands he felt compelled to try the faucet several times to see if it was closed. He had a problem about bathing and cleanliness: he could not decide whether or not to take a bath and sometimes went without one longer than a week, all the while feeling guilty and being afraid that he had an offensive odor.

A cause of great distress to him was his compulsion to telephone people repeatedly during the day or night and to make sure after the call that he had not left the receiver off the hook. He had to return again and again to convince himself that it was in place. These toilet and telephone obsessions made him exceedingly miserable.

He presented a clear and characteristic picture of the compulsive neurotic: wanting to be an anti-social, defiant child in every respect and at the same time being compelled to model behavior. All his symptoms expressed both these tendencies, in addition to serving as agents of self-punishment for his asocial drives. For many months he suffered intensely from self-criticism, but could not understand why he felt as he did. The reason for his suffering was "isolated". It was therefore difficult for him to produce free associations, the progress of analysis was impeded and in addition he was prevented from *feeling* his relationship with the persons whom his compulsions concerned. It took a long time for him to realize that his compulsion to telephone people (mostly men) meant on the one hand to seek dependence (especially on men). It also expressed aggression towards women, derived from early feelings of aggression towards the frustrating mother; and at the same time it expressed his desire to call mother, to obtain reassurance from her. Additional factors in the telephone obsession were strong aggressive impulses against his employer, by whom he was very much intimidated, and whom he called sometimes four or five times in the course of the night. (The employer was usually in his office at night). The patient used all kinds of excuses for the calls, all directed at impressing upon his boss his obedience, dependence, industry, and ambition. Another means of trying to make a favorable impression (and also gain attention) was his use of long words and involved phrases. He was proud of his ability to weave them into his literary work. He wanted to be admired for his knowledge and for his scholarly vocabulary; to draw attention to these he spoke with a careful enunciation and a particular inflexion. This practise satisfied his vanity, but as it was also a substitute gratification for his exhibitionistic tendencies, feelings of rivalry, and desire for erotic pleasures, it had the additional effect at times of inhibiting him in his work. The accomplishment of his work meant proof of potency (sexual ability) to him. On a still deeper level it was equated with anal productions (erotization of thoughts and speech).

His obsession that the telephone receiver be on the hook had many determinants. One was undoing his tendency to call, which was an aggressive act. It also symbolically expressed the inactivity of his penis; it was not making any calls on women, therefore he was being a good boy and not rebelling against father's prohibitions. This obsession started to subside and later was eliminated when the patient was able to begin to follow a more positive, adult line of development; when he began to be active instead of regressive and dependent. He became less afraid of his employer, accomplished a separation from his wife and for the first time had his own apartment.

His concern about the toilet bowl being flushed and the water faucet shut off, led directly back to his early childhood memories. It became evident that he was struggling with problems arising from his early childhood attachment to his mother, his desire for her, fear of his father and hostility towards him. From earliest childhood up to puberty he had many opportunities of seeing his mother's nude body and also his little sister's, as the two children were given their baths together. His strong hostility and feeling of frustration date from the time the sister entered the scene.   The wish to be dirty carried the desire to have his mother give him a bath, as she did in childhood, to give him her attention, thus getting her away from father and sister.   For all these desires he was compelled to punish himself and the suffering he endured as a result of these compulsive actions served his need for expiation of hostile tendencies.   The obsessions about the toilet and faucet expressed the same contradiction: being a naughty spiteful boy, yet obeying superego commands and being an obedient, good boy.   The toilet bowl also symbolized the female genitals, referring to mother and his early observations of her nude body.   A flushed toilet bowl meant nullification of the unconscious wish to impregnate women, which had its origin in the early Œdipus wishes.   The dry faucet equalled abstinence from phallic pleasures, urination and seminal emissions.

These obsessions were also connected with the problem of seeing or touching the female genitals.   The toilet and faucet substituted for his curiosity about the female genital, an interest that was outstanding in his early childhood and also in the early puberty period.   The obsessions also served to isolate (and thereby eliminate) the discomfort and guilt which would accompany his preoccupation with the vagina. He felt embarrassed and ashamed of discussing these problems when they were related to his current experiences with women, after he had left his wife.   He showed attempts to make analysis an obsession in order to avoid discussing his feelings about sex when he became more aware of such feelings.

The closed faucet further expressed undoing an extremely hostile unconscious desire to exterminate everybody. The repressed thought which eventually came to the surface was that if he let the faucet run there would be no water left in the reservoirs and people would die of thirst. Therefore he had to counteract this wish by means of the ritual of repeatedly trying the faucet to make sure it was closed. At times he felt compelled to leave a party or the theatre in the middle of a performance in order to come home and ascertain that the water was not running or that the telephone was on the hook. He had to be alert in his defenses against his repressed aggressions. His ambivalence was constant because of the threat of recurring hate, which he tried to counteract with good behavior.

The great extent to which his sex life carried anal-sadistic tendencies became more and more evident as analysis progressed. In his marriage his sexual intercourse was isolated from his feelings. It was automatic, without tender or pleasurable sensations. After he divorced his wife and began for the first time to have pleasurable sensations with other women, he described his previous intercourse with his wife in derogatory, obscene, anal terms. He said that he had used her as a toilet, that he had felt only the desire to attack and soil her, and so forth. At times when he attempted sexual intercourse with his new friend, he felt confused, as if he did not know where the female genitals were. He himself remarked that this was rather a curious feeling, because he had had sexual intercourse with his wife innumerable times, always successfully, and he never had experienced such confusion. It seemed to him that he never had looked at or touched his wife's genitals and that he had not looked at his friend's genitals either. He had fondled her, however, and tried at times to put his finger in her vagina. In general he was more interested than ever in his sexual partner's reaction. But with the gradual development of his masculine sexual interest, attraction to women, and greater enjoyment of sex, he developed anxiety concerning subsequent attachment to the woman.

His obsessional indecisiveness was very much in evidence in his relationship to women. His continual feeling of doubt and his ambivalence basically concerned instinctual drives, especially sexual desires. The state of indecision was an endless source of torture to him. In every situation, the conflict between strivings for adulthood and remaining a child was present, thus he forced others to decide for him.

In his new relationships with women, especially after he experienced thrilling sensations and felt a real desire to be loved, the old pattern of castration fears again began to disturb his adjustment. The fear of impregnating his partner preoccupied him. The dangers of sexual intercourse, hurting the woman, making her sick through pregnancy, all these thoughts distracted him whenever he had a rendezvous. He recalled the agonizing feelings he had when his wife was pregnant. The compunctions about her suffering caused him to imagine similar situations with his new acquaintances. Obsessive ideas of killing the woman through pregnancy made him feel that coitus was a sadistic attack upon the woman, and that he must refrain. On the one hand he was constantly excited sexually, having frequent erections; on the other hand he was convinced that he could not be attractive, women could not like him because of his looks. He wanted constant reassurance that father's threats at puberty about masturbation were untrue. (It will be recalled that at puberty when he asked about his erections, the father warned him against masturbating.)

At this period he produced a few interesting dreams which indicated the progress he had made.

"I am fighting, take a hell of a beating, but stand up". With all the associations, it boiled down to what the patient seemed to think about his progress: "I am more up than down at the present".

"A child is being killed. His head is being mashed because something was growing out of the neck, like a pimple, like a penis, that exploded and killed the child".

This dream reviews in a few short phrases his castration fear and actually his whole neurosis: the enormous fear of his childhood genital aims, fear of his aggression (exploding) from which he had to escape.

Another dream he reported: "I had a terrible fight with father and told him he is no better than I. I asked him why he feels so high and mighty and told him he is responsible for all my trouble".

In this period of gradual adjustment the patient's fantasies and dreams were still sadistically colored. However, through them he expressed real wishes and desires, in contrast to the dreams and fantasies of the early phase of analysis which were all of an escape nature.

The more progressive his sexual drives became, the greater were his defensive efforts to revert to the old regressive anal tendencies. The following dream is a good illustration:

> "I wanted to find a lake to swim in. When I got there the lake was full of mud; the water was dried out and under the mud it was all like feces. I went into a latrine. I wore a pair of trunks. There was a row of toilets. I walked barefoot; there was urine on the floor and I was disgusted. Then I wanted to find the lake again. I saw it in the distance; I approached it but did not go in."

Around the time of the dream he had been going out frequently with women but was still afraid to accept the responsibility that sexual intercourse involves. The dream expresses the conflict between his tendency to regress to the level of anal pleasures and the gradually strengthening desire for heterosexual experience (the lake). After a sexual experience he would use all kinds of abusive anal expressions to describe his partner and intercourse itself. But such regressive attempts quickly subsided. The ritualistic preoccupations and magical gestures which were intended to undo his destructive wishes and also to save himself, the fear of really feeling and expressing his aggression in an adult manner, were slowly replaced by a more mature attitude, and he was able to face his reality problems, above all his genitality, as an adult.

Therapy is a very slow process and cannot be hastened by means of any special technique. Active interference has no beneficial effect. On the contrary, it may add to the material of which the patient forms his obsessions. A suggestion may be interpreted by the patient as positive advice or even as a command. When he realizes that nothing has changed through his efforts to carry out the suggestion, he takes it as proof of the ineffectiveness of analysis and the analyst. Activity on the part of the analyst thus creates new waves of hostility, repentance and self-punishment. In treating compulsion neuroses the analyst must go very slowly, giving the patient time to go through his periods of depression and doubt. After such periods the patient is amenable to interpretation and is able to acquire some insight into his previous depressive feelings. During the time that he is acutely upset he is unable to see the connection between his actions and feelings because the torturing obsessions inhibit clear thinking or reality functioning.

To his unconscious, thoughts and feelings equal actions; the obsessive thoughts substitute for actions. Until the patient realizes that the two are not the same, he cannot indulge in thoughts or fantasies without feeling guilty and punishing himself. He must dare to recognize the latent meaning of his obsessive thoughts and compulsions and come to understand how they originated. Then the meaning of the symptoms must be investigated in the light of his experiences.

All analysts agree that it takes an extremely long time to break the obsessional system. This is accomplished through the transference relationship, in which the patient gradually learns to evaluate other external object relationships and reality situations. The transference will be a hostile one; the patient will discover that because of his sadism he fears emotional involvements and that his object relationships are therefore weak.

The first therapeutic success is achieved when the patient perceives the meaning of the threat which is causing him panic and is able to react to it. The reaction will be expressed in hostility towards the analyst, reviving and discharging aggression and rebellion which were first related to the patient's super-ego, later involved everybody and created his enormous sense of guilt, which he has been continually attempting to appease through both logic and magic. (With one part of his personality he works magic, still believing in the omnipotence of thoughts and gestures; the other part rages against carrying out such nonsensical impulses.) These two parts are clearly distinguishable: one striving to regress to the narcissistic magical period of development, while the other continues to be logical and maintains contact with reality.

The patient's display of his ever-present aggression paralleled by desires for guidance and love must be encouraged, not censured. In this way the ideas and verbal productions concerning the analyst will be *felt* by the patient. His repetitive compulsive preoccupations, which were a means of escape from such feelings will thus be reduced. Through the re-direction of the aggression to the objects which originally provoked it, the patient learns to dare to speak without fearing the consequences. Then the need to isolate feelings from intellect lessens and his fear of accepting his aggression diminishes. After he accepts his sadistic object relationships, he no longer feels the need to fight off emotional involvements and he slowly learns to accept tender feelings as well.

This patient's progress and imminent recovery were reflected in his reaction to the death of President Roosevelt. He had always liked to read the casualty lists and stated, when advanced in treatment, that it always gave him a secret pleasure. He felt that he would gain from the deaths of others because there would be less men in the world to compete with. However, towards the end of analysis he began to feel genuinely fond of some people. It came as a great surprise to him (and it was actually the first time in his life) that he had a feeling of sadness and loss with no conflicting feelings whatsoever, at the death of the late President.

Chapter *VII*

CHARACTER NEUROSIS

Usually patients come for analytic treatment because of symptoms which cause them pain and suffering. The type of patients referred to as having character difficulties generally come to analysis because of feelings of inferiority and inadequacy which prevent them from having a harmonious social life. At times, and under certain circumstances, of course, every one of us may feel inferior and inadequate, but with these people the feelings are present to a high degree under all conditions. Their stereotyped reactions, rigidity, and inability to adapt themselves to situations ultimately lead to unhappiness.

Our investigations trace the entire character development back to early childhood, as if a film were being reeled off in reverse. Peculiarities acquired in childhood exert influence upon the conduct of the adult. There is indisputable evidence that neurotic symptoms of adulthood correspond to these peculiarities in childhood behavior. That does not mean, however, that irregularities in a child's behavior always become neurotic symptoms.

One may ask why unusual behavior patterns develop in one person to a greater degree than in another, or why they become so pronounced in some cases that they lead not only to a clearly differentiated personality but even to the formation of a specific character type. Constitutional and environmental factors together provide the clue to differences in character development. Through psychoanalytic investigation one learns to appreciate the importance of the influence of the environment on the growing individual. Translating environment into parental attitudes, one learns to recognize the parents' influence on the child, and to perceive the patterns of reaction formed by the child in the course of his development, as a result of that influence.

Character difficulties are always the result of poor adjustment in early childhood, which has come about through a series of more or less permanent imprints on the young ego, through identification with persons of immediate importance in the environment. The earliest and most important identifications take place in connection with struggles to overcome instinctual drives. The examples set by parents and educators are absorbed by the child and form that part of the personality which is called the superego, the critical faculty. Among its many functions it helps mould the child's character, at times prompting the child to be like its parents, at other times influencing him to be their opposites. In the healthy child both tendencies are present. The tendency to become the extreme opposite of one's parents can become dominant as a result of an unhappy childhood. When this occurs, the person becomes the type described as "the reactive character", having inhibitions in social or private life, (as, for example, ascetic behavior) although they may have made an outward adjustment and adapted themselves to society. In these individuals the character system is built up against primitive impulses and excludes them completely.

People with character difficulties are all strongly narcissistic and extremely afraid of neurotic symptoms and depression. Their organized defenses are consciously arranged to maintain a constant resistance; outstanding is the transference resistance which influences their attitude towards any change in their behavior. Their superficial, steady stream of conversation is also carefully planned with a view to avoiding free association. If even a slight change in behavior is pointed out, if they are led to see that they are doing better in certain relationships they may refuse to admit it. On such occasions the transference resistance becomes clearly apparent. The strength and depth of repression in these cases makes difficult any release of anxiety and guilt, and thus inhibits for a long period the development of a positive transference. The armor with which they have covered themselves in the course of development in order to avoid emotional involvements is nearly impenetrable, hence they exhibit "negative therapeutic reactions" to analysis.

The analyst represents the parental images who are remembered mainly for their frustrating attitudes and deprivations. Therefore the patient constantly resists analysis even when he clearly understands the interpretations of his resistance. The appearance of physical symptoms and general feelings of discomfort will be the first signs that analysis is taking effect. The dissection of these transitory symptoms will begin to create in the patient the ability to evaluate feelings. These first feelings of which he becomes aware are anxiety concerning his health, then resentment and aggression (transference manifestations). They mark the inception of emotional experience and gradually lead to the uncovering of the carefully repressed past experiences and reactions to them.

The following case, which I analyzed about fifteen years ago, and the healthy adjustment of which I have since had the opportunity to observe, illustrates many of the difficulties with which one has to deal in character neuroses, and also shows some technical aspects of treatment. The patient was a young man in his early twenties who came for treatment because for several years he had been unable to make decisions in matters that were important to his profession, and at the time he came to analysis, he was faced with the dilemma of deciding whether or not to marry.

He was somewhat taciturn, composed in his bearing, and his face bore a morose expression. He led an extensive social life, but could not understand why people liked him or sought his company; nor could he understand why he was commended for the quality of his work. His doubts about his friends and his own ability were not based on external reality, because he was always ready to do favors, to give advice and to help any co-worker who turned to him. This behavior, however, was somewhat automatic and superficial. Actually, he was extremely tense, and behind the tension were signs of deep anxiety. In the course of analysis, when he had become able to recognize certain emotions and to accept them as his own, his description of his feelings was that he was "burning inside" and that the burning made him "a shallow and empty person". His emotional problems, centering around indecision, became so pressing when he contemplated marriage that he was forced to seek help. From that point, the entire problem of making decisions was followed back to its origin, the problems of childhood and the Œdipal situation. He was unable to make a decision regarding his masculinity striving; the result was a general indecisiveness. His struggles began with a fight against dependence upon his mother, and, following that line of development, he strove to resist depending on any woman for pleasure or gratification.

It took a long while in his analysis for him to recognize that he actually had rich and colorful fantasies, and that to prevent indulgence in them he surrounded himself with books of all types. He kept three or four volumes beside the bed so that he could read if he happened to awake during the night. The fantasies from which he tried to escape were sadistically colored and all were of a frank sexual nature. For instance, he fantasied having a very big strong penis and raping women. When using enemas, he sometimes pretended that he was a girl and that the enema stick in his anus was someone's finger. His calm exterior covered distrust and aggression and his indecisiveness was also related to avoiding the acceptance of responsibility for his fantasies, which he could not consciously tolerate because of the sadism they expressed.

This patient had gone through many experiences that children are generally spared. He clearly remembered being circumcized at the age of four. His father held him while the doctor performed the operation. On this experience was built the feeling of resentment and hatred for his father. He thought that his penis had become less sensitive to friction because of the operation and he believed that had it not been performed he would have achieved greater satisfaction from masturbation.

A fellatio experience with a cousin at the age of six was another vivid memory. The patient's mother discovered them and threatened to take him to the hospital and have his penis cut off. His fear of castration made him cling to the fantasy of a female penis. Observation of his mother and adult sister gave rise to the belief that the only difference between male and female genitals was that in the female they were covered with hair.

He was the only boy in a large family. Although he was unable to exhibit any love for his mother, strong incestuous feelings about her were revealed in the course of analysis.

At the age of eight or nine, when he had already observed the copulation of animals, he asked his father about coitus. His father laughingly replied that only animals do it. Knowing that his father was not telling the truth made him very angry and he reacted by masturbating. He recalls that from then on he always masturbated when he was angered by his parents or by his sisters.

At puberty he was seduced by a relative and then was afraid she might disclose the incident. After this experience he masturbated more actively. He began to use enemas to relieve constipation. Preoccupation with his bowel functions also served as another form of masturbation. Sometimes when giving himself enemas he felt sexually excited, had erections, and seminal emissions.

Strong bisexual tendencies were obvious in his dreams. Homosexual fantasies served as an escape from heterosexual activities and were based on his disappointment in and disgust with women.

The fear of growing up was incorporated in his fear of making a decision; the former was reactivated in analysis and appeared in his resistance to treatment. He fought signs of positive transference because of his fear of dependence. On the other hand, he always demanded advice and guidance. Strongly narcissistic as he was, he did not want to give any affection; at the same time he constantly behaved so agreeably in his social life that he was liked by everyone. He could, however, find no pleasure in that success because of the underlying distrust of people and hostility towards them. He had to be very much afraid of his aggression because of the original castration threats which were still vivid in his unconscious, and because the aggression against those who administered the threats (mother, father, and sisters), was accompanied by feelings of guilt. He was deeply concerned about the members of his family and about their well-being. It took him a long time to perceive and accept the fact that the reason for this concern was, in truth, a selfish one; namely that he did not want to be bothered worrying about their illness. He always wanted to know that his parents were in good health and he became very upset at their slightest complaint. It was extremely difficult for the patient to recognize his hostility against his parents, his death wishes, his rages about their past injustices and their present "coldness".

His general attitude toward everyone was deep distrust behind superficial compliance. It was a sign of considerable progress when he could argue at his place of work and demand that certain suggestions of his be carried out; or when he could refuse to do certain favors, which previously he had been ready to do without a second thought, only later on realizing that he had been taken advantage of.

The parents' extreme severity, improper handling of his emotional reactions, and failure to understand his moods in childhood were responsible for his characteristic type of reaction in adulthood. The superego, which has such an important function in moulding the child's character, was of a type with which he could not identify himself in a healthy manner. He was wronged in childhood many times. He did not dare to make demands; that became a strong pattern of reaction, and he could not demand even when he was justified. In analysis, when he gained insight into his problems and the need to change his reactions, he constantly repeated, "It is too late to change".

In another volume [1] I referred briefly to a case of the same type. The patient was a psychiatrist who had become more and more dissatisfied with his mode of living, with his tendency to be too impulsive at times, at others too deeply concerned about his behavior and about his friends' reactions to him. Emotional

[1] "Character Formation." *Psychoanalysis Today*, ed. by S. Lorand, International University Press, 1944, New York.

factors in the behavior of his patients, whom he treated according to his theoretical knowledge of psychoanalytic principles, he readily recognized; however, he constantly refused to accept them in relation to his own behavior. He analyzed his patients' dreams, understood them, and interpreted them correctly. He perceived the relationship between their early childhood patterns and their Œdipus conflicts, but dreams of his own which clearly pointed to his relationships with his family members and his Œdipal situation, he ridiculed and rejected. When in the advanced stage of a long-lasting analysis his aggression against his parents became obvious, he constantly reiterated a fear of going crazy. A few dreams of this period will be instructive in showing why he was afraid of recognizing and accepting his repressed thoughts and feelings:

"I went insane and strangled my brother. I was an adult in the dreams, I felt madness and terror."

Or another dream:

"The worker in the Clinic said: 'We have to be careful not to bring out a negative transference'. I told the worker that this was exactly what we had to bring out in therapy."

This second dream clearly depicts his attitude toward analysis. In the clinic with his own patients he could instruct others and follow the therapeutic rules to mobilize feelings and interpret reactions. But nearly up to the time this dream appeared, he had repressed all feeling in the transference relation. In the light of his associations this dream was a warning against bringing out his own negative feelings. His rebellion was always accompanied by guilt, and fear arose whenever a rebellious attitude was sensed by him. On occasions when he came to analysis in a taxi, he gave the driver his own address. After three years of analysis he made the following slip: when intending to say, "In my analysis, etc.," he said, "In my analysis of you". Under the mask of outward compliance he still had that much resistance.

It took three years for the patient to arrive at this phase where he began to realize how much aggression he had and that his panic served to prevent its breaking through.

It took that long for him to understand that his superego (conscience) did not permit him to have pleasures, that his sense of guilt made him feel undeserving of them. He constantly punished himself to satisfy both his conscious sense of guilt, and also his unconscious need for punishment.

With women patients having character difficulties, the problem is the same. Their anxiety, their deep distrust and fear of dependence have their roots in the Œdipal relationships, and they experience difficulties in their sexual life as a result of early dependence and frustrations. In relationships with men they react to intercourse at times with a satisfactory orgasm, at others with a violent climax and sometimes are completely unable to reach an orgasm. In analysis a number of seemingly masculine character attributes will be discovered, although the patients may have a very feminine appearance, and exhibit feminine behavior. Intellectually, however, they invariably want to prove that they are equal or superior to men. They very often choose a weaker partner in marriage. They mobilize all their intellectual forces (intellectualizing the emotional process) to resist all changes which the treatment effects because they fear relinquishing the borrowed masculine attitude. Sexual gratification is achieved not from a man but solely from a penis, to which the man is merely an appendix. In the process of analysis, their attitude changes slowly to one of wanting to be gratified by the man as well as the penis, but a long drawn-out struggle must be weathered before such a period is reached. A few dreams of a female patient with character difficulties may illustrate the type of resistance women use to deny the feminine role and the sexual relationship with men.

"I am in Verona in the house of Romeo and Juliet. I am on the balcony and under the balcony Bernard Shaw is standing. We have a good time in an intellectual discussion."

Intellectuality was emphasized in the dream because of her habit of intellectualizing whenever emotional attitudes were in evidence. This dream referred to her deep Œdipal attachment to father. To hide the incestuously erotic feelings she makes the relationship with the father image a purely intellectual one.

Another dream:

"A tailor is fitting me. I am unhappy about the texture. Then he rents me a room. I take it, but people make too much noise and I am unhappy and sorry that I took the room."

In association, the latter dream was understood to relate to analysis and the conflict about accepting a new type of behavior (new suit). She refuses whatever the analyst offers her because there are too many other patients who share his attention. She also mentioned changing analysts because she was dissatisfied with the results. On a deeper level, the entire dream refers to her sexual problems. She does not want to accept what analysis aims to accomplish, "femininity", because of fear of her desire to have many men (too much noise).

The bisexual tendencies of this type of patient also come to the fore in the analytical process and the penis envy and penis wishes continually reappear in their dreams and fantasies as a defense against a possible feminine attitude. Another female patient had curious mixed fantasies about the analyst. At times he shrank in size until he dropped through a hole. (Her constant wish was to humiliate and trap him). In another fantasy he grew larger and larger and she was very much frightened. This fantasy referred to her fear of male superiority.

At the age of five she had seen her father's genital and never forgot the shock she experienced at the sight of it. Also from the age of five and up, she saw her brother's penis and at six, her brother told her how babies were made: "The man's big thing is stuck in the lady." At the age of thirteen, when she began to menstruate, she was horrified by fantasies of penises flying around and into her mouth. For a long time she refused to see that her aggression against men and fear of them were the cause of her periodic inability to reach an orgasm. At a period of her analysis when she was on good terms with her male friends, she had the following dream:

"Many of us are sleeping together, men and women. A man reaches under my skirt, puts his finger in a hole in my panties and up to my vagina. I get mad, punch him with both fists. I am going upstairs with a woman (a relative). I am sexually excited at the thought that I will be with her."

She had begun to develop a fear that the men would become attached to her and would suffer because she could not love them. This pressing and often voiced fear was an overcompensation for her unconscious wish to hurt them.

The outstanding difficulty in the therapy of character neuroses is the fixed type of emotional reaction which is used as resistance to change. Therefore, the first step is to recognize these tendencies in the patient, explore them and relate them to early childhood difficulties. These patients became spiteful and defiant in childhood as a result of the overseverity of the superego. They became obstinate because of unjust treatment by the parents. Cases with character difficulty display a type of rigidity which hinders them from manifesting their feelings to anyone. To break up that rigidity and mobilize their feelings is the most important problem of technique. The more defensive they are, the greater will be the rigidity, which follows as a result of the general pattern of behavior. The patients themselves state that they want to avoid all kinds of feelings; they do not want to become involved. The desire to avoid emotional involvements is due to deep anxiety and fear of repetition of frustration which attended the attachments of earlier years. Therefore emotional reactions are covered by powerful resistance. They accept analytic theory and use it to understand others, but refuse to apply it to themselves. They theorize extensively, instead of engaging in introspection, an activity of which they are particularly afraid. Their resistance is well rationalized and though good theoretical knowledge of analysis is acquired, they are irritated by the interpretations and at times laugh at them, declaring that they have no unconscious. In their analysis a stubborn attempt is made to recreate the childhood situation and to prove that they are being treated unjustly. They try to provoke the analyst by every means at their command in order to disrupt the treatment and prove to themselve that they are misunderstood, disliked, and mistreated. The analyst must be extremely tolerant and must communicate to the patient the understanding that under no circumstances will he (the therapist) discontinue the treatment.

Another mode of resistance employed by this type of patient is forgetting what has been discussed in analysis; forgetting dreams and accepted interpretations, or some statement they have made but do not like to face, and then accusing the analyst of having confused the material of other patients. At other times they insist that they have mentioned incidents in analysis which they never did bring up, and further, they frequently are taciturn and poor in producing associations. For the most part the defense mechanisms are not different from those employed in other neuroses; however this type of patient exhibits many more variations. The most outstanding is the attempt to intellectualize instead of permitting themselves any feelings. They go to extremes of self-criticism and self-abuse. Naturally, it all covers strong fear of criticism which makes them take as a personal attack every interpretation that concerns them as an individual. At other times they present themselves as helpless, weak, and inferior. This is the defense against accepting responsibilities, deciding about an attitude or action, or even determining how they should feel in certain situations. Another defense is the attempt to control the analysis and the analyst. To this end they often provoke arguments, and may succeed in drawing the analyst into a controversy which is then taken as proof of the analyst's weakness and the consequent worthlessness of the whole treatment. Sometimes they try to control the analytical situation by playful attitudes. That approach, however, is not as common as preparing pitfalls for the analyst by provocation and arguments, through which they also want to prove their intellectual equality if not superiority to the analyst. In their intellectual achievements one usually finds that women patients with character difficulties have gone further than the average man. In some of the female patients with character neuroses, the striving for intellectual superiority over the male began as competition with the male members of their families, by whom they felt oppressed in childhood. In reality these women have all had a bad environment, were made to feel inferior, were ridiculed by brothers or father, and tormented in various ways. It is only natural for them to harbor strong feelings of rebellion, resentment, and strong castrating tendencies as a result of these abuses, which have the added effect of causing them to strive for equality with men.

In male patients with character neuroses, the same mechanisms are at work. In their analysis previously repressed childhood memories will point to their having been mistreated continually, so that later in life when they know intellectually that they are in the right, they still feel doubtful and do not dare demand what is rightfully theirs. This feeling of being in the wrong and being oppressed is of course charged with aggression. Equally strong charges of guilt from the early childhood period are also carried along, causing fear of displaying any decisive feelings since they might reactivate the early conflicts about wrong and right, love and hate, relating to the parents or parent-substitutes. Theoretically, these people can be described as having been terrified by their superego against which strong rebellion and guilt arose but were repressed. One never fails to find traumatic experiences in the pre-Œdipal or Œdipal phase of development of this type of patient.

Generally, character traits and special types of behavior serve as a protection against the development of symptoms or neurotic illness. I mentioned above that therapeutic results can only be obtained if the neurotic illness and its symptoms manifest themselves. In the process of analysis that will surely take place and through the symptoms the patient learns to tolerate pain and cope with fear of distress. These people have to become ill in order to be treated. Their typical, characteristic behavior patterns and reactions must be broken up and the anxiety at the thought of experiencing distress or any feeling of discomfort, must become the object of analysis. Patients of this type want to be advised and guided in their decisions; they want to *learn* not to be *treated*. They are willing to gain intellectual insight into their character traits and habits, may even concede that they experience some discomfort or degree of unhappiness at not being able to make decisions, admit that they want help, but refuse to consider their difficulties an illness.

It took years for one of my patients of that type to accept as neurotic manifestations her symptoms of alternating diarrhea and constipation, burning sensations in the rectum, etc. She persisted in treating them as physiological. The physicians whom she consulted could find no physiological causes for her complaints. All they were able to do was to prescribe diets, suppositories, or enemas. Analyzing these symptoms, discussing their possible connection with real emotional and sexual experiences finally effected changes in her general attitude toward physical pain, i.e. her fears of it were reduced. Thus her fixed type of reaction to physical symptoms was altered. Then the change in her attitude was broadened to reach her fixed type of emotional reaction in general. Her preoccupation with physical symptoms and their supposed physiological origin had made her very refractory in analysis. Only when this extreme preoccupation with physical symptoms was weakened could she be induced to focus her attention on her actual behavior and deep unhappiness. In order to reduce characterological difficulties, analysis must first handle the transitory symptoms which the patient develops in the course of treatment.

Clinical observation is of great help in analyzing those character difficulties which serve as a shield against being emotionally disturbed. When the shield is pierced, the patient slowly comes to recognize the fact that his forceful adjustment is a counterpart of poor adjustment in childhood, and that the difficulties he experiences in business and society (and for that matter in family life as well) are a result of parental imprints made during the early stages of his development. One finds that the parents or those entrusted with the upbringing of these individuals made very few or no sacrifices and *adjusted themselves very little to the child's demands.* In the childhood struggle to change habits, adopt new ones, adjust to new environments, school, friends, and the like, these patients received very little help from parents and siblings.

In the transference relationship, they endeavor to satisfy all the frustrated childhood desires. They want the analyst to adjust to them: they exert pressure upon him to change rules and regulations, and he does at times have to modify his approach in order to overcome the difficulties which these patients present. Their refusal to comply with the fundamental rules of free association, their denial of unconscious motivations, and so forth, must be recognized as symptoms and must be treated accordingly. Pressure or persuasion may be very upsetting to the patient. Analysis under these difficult circumstances which the patient creates is far from an easy task. Ferenczi's advice to use the method of "forced fantasies" is of great help in these cases. It is surprising to what extent this can mobilize stagnant analysis.

The objective in character analysis is the same as in any other analysis: namely to make the patient recognize and properly evaluate the total structure of his personality, and the elements which have made it what it is. The results may not be as striking as in other neuroses, but these patients do learn better control of their impulsive reactions and adjust themselves more easily to reality.

Chapter VIII
NEUROTIC DEPRESSION [1]

In discussing various technical approaches in the treatment of the neuroses, mention was made of special modes of treating patients with character difficulties. Atypical technical approaches combined with guidance, suggestions, and attempts at re-education play an even more prominent role in the treatment of depressive states. The ego of these patients shows a low degree of stability. General psychotherapeutic methods have to be freely employed in certain stages of the analysis in order to foster the development of a transference. This in turn creates a certain amount of self-confidence in the patient, thereby promoting the special aim of therapy which is to strengthen the ego feelings in order to create a better reality functioning.

For illustration of the varied and complicated technical devices which one must employ with this type of patient, a case history is herewith presented, the symptoms of which indicate a classical anorexia nervosa. Behind the symptom complex, however, the deeply involved personality difficulties were those typical of neurotic depression.

The patient was in her early twenties. She had been under medical care for many years. Prior to her analysis, she had been for two weeks in a university clinic and was sent away without any sugges-

[1] The first part of the case history presented in this chapter is a condensation of a paper entitled "Anorexia Nervosa" which appeared in *Psychosomatic Medicine*, Vol. V, No. 3, 1943. The second part, dealing with the depressive features, is published here for the first time.

tion for medical treatment. In the clinic, she had been receiving injections for amenorrhea.

The family physician referred her to me with complaints characteristic of the anorexia nervosa symptom complex: disgust with food, loss of appetite and taste for food, gagging at the sight of it, dryness of mouth, periodic vomiting. All were aggravated if she tried to force herself to eat. Accompanying symptoms were excruciating pains in the epigastrium and lower abdomen and periodic amenorrhea. She also complained of increased growth of hair on the torso, face, lips, arms, and thighs; occasional constipation; feeling of cold and depression most of the time. Her symptoms can be divided into three main groups: first, peculiar reactions to food; second, disturbances in bowel functions; and third, menstrual disorders and amenorrhea.

All these symptoms had been present off and on for about ten years. Her illness started at twelve when she had crying spells and feelings of depression. She lost weight from time to time because of disgust with food, but gained easily after the symptom subsided. Before she was twelve she had had many emotional setbacks, felt unhappy, and had difficulties in school. She liked her teachers and was a good student, but was afraid of the other children and hated them because they laughed and played while she felt unable to join them. She would go home from school in a nasty temper. In high school the same situation prevailed; she always had the feeling of not belonging with other children. She had always been fussy about eating. After every meal she used to lie on her stomach across a chair to get relief from pressure. However, the disturbance did not become very severe until she was twelve. Just about that time the family moved from one neighborhood to another. She did not like the people and told her mother she hated the new home. From then on she was moody, cried a great deal, and lost her appetite. Menses started at fourteen but were never regular. Because of frequent abdominal pains, appendectomy was performed when she was eighteen but proved to be unnecessary. She had also undergone a plastic nose operation to improve her appearance. This was done without her parents' previous knowledge and before she started analysis.

When she began treatment with me she was going through one of her periods of depression and crying spells. For days she was unable to eat solid food. At night, when everyone was asleep, she would go to the icebox and eat lightly. She attributed her condition at that time to steadily growing tension and resentment toward her mother. She felt that her mother was neglecting the home for her social engagements which kept her away most of the day. This state of affairs was nothing new, but it seemed at that time to be growing worse. It infuriated the patient because it made her ashamed of having such a mother and because her father was neglected.

From the outset of the analysis her behavior was childish and her carriage, voice, mode of speech, were all playful and coquettish. During this time she was not able to bear much frustration and so was given every freedom possible to encourage the display of her feelings. In the first few months appointments were changed according to her wishes and ingenuity was needed to keep her from running away in the middle of an analytical hour because of intense rage and unhappiness. She was on the verge of quitting treatment whenever she became enraged by her mother, father, or sister.

When she was in a bad temper with her mother she felt like choking her. She described her mother as a cold woman who was always nagging and shouting at father and the children, particularly at her. She accused her mother of neglecting the children and said she could not believe her mother's protestations of affection. Her mother told her that she nursed her for five months, wanted to do so longer but that the patient refused to take the breast. Almost in the same breath the mother expressed her disgust at the act of suckling babies. The patient commented: "Probably I did not want to take something that was not given with love. Kids sense love that early, the same way dogs can tell who the people are who love them."

She complained that her mother, who was a simple woman with little cultivation, was always impatient with her. This was taken as proof that her mother did not want her. Then too, her mother often cursed and ridiculed her, expressing the hope that the patient would have children like herself so that she might know the torture she had caused her mother. Along with feelings of hostility the patient felt compunction and guilt. She was sarcastic and termed every word she uttered a "worm". She was constantly resentful and aggressive and at the same time suffered guilt, pains, crying spells, and depression.

The mother's attitude towards her created constant anxiety in childhood with the result that she was shy, retiring, morose, and she brooded. As a child she became convinced that her mother was dangerous because she displayed varying attitudes towards all the children. Towards her father, whom she considered maltreated by mother, the patient was at times sympathetic, but ambivalence developed very early. She distrusted both parents, and as a result could not express tender emotions. She schooled herself to appear composed so as to conceal her need for dependence and parental love. Thus she attempted to spare herself disappointment.

In her early childhood she also felt unwanted because her parents had wanted a boy. When the boy was born she was extremely jealous. As he grew older and was admired for his appearance she felt ugly and inferior. Her mother had told her that when she was two years old she (the mother) was ashamed to take her on the street for fear people would comment on her skinny, ugly child. The patient frequently questioned her mother as to whether she was a step-child and was disappointed by the negative reply.

She repeatedly expressed the thought that parents should be dead before children are born. She went on to say: "I felt I wanted only to hate, then I felt I wanted only to love: then I didn't want anything". She said she could not eat because she hated everybody around her at home. Her mother threw the food at her and she wanted it served appetizingly. Mother repeated to her many times that "mothers should never be born because they suffer so much".

Her relationship to her father was strongly ambivalent and there was a long struggle in analysis until she reached the point of being able to be in his presence without conflict. He always came home from business in a bad temper. He was domineering, argumentative at home, and cruel in his business dealings. Nevertheless, he could be more tender at times than her mother. She recognized in herself certain resemblances to her father: critical and sarcastic attitudes, tone of voice, and expression of the eyes.

He once forced her, in the presence of other people, to eat eggs which she promptly vomited on him, soiling his suit. He never seemed satisfied with her, always interfered, telling her what to eat and what to do. He taught her to be stiff and formal in his presence. Once, as she served her father a glass of water, she thought "I hope you choke on it". Then in guilt she tried to nullify it by thinking "I hope you don't choke on it". Such conflicting thoughts about him tortured her.

At other times, however, she was sympathetic towards him. As analysis progressed, her thoughts and fantasies about him showed increasing confusion: concern, contempt, attachment, and rejection. She was jealous of both father and brother whose identity she often confused in her dreams. She feared that her brother might rape her.

The emotional problem caused by her father remained active. It was not until the end of the second year of analysis that she was able to sit through a meal with him. When the meal was over, she was at ease and relaxed, whereas previously, dining with him sometimes brought on abdominal pains, stomach symptoms, and eating difficulties that lasted for days.

Rivalry with the sister from earliest childhood was an important factor in her illness. Before her brother was born she was aware of the partiality shown her older sister, particularly by her father. Her mother mentioned many times that when the patient was born, her sister, then over two years of age, wanted to kill her with a big stick and throw her out of the window. At the age of two the patient kept herself meticulously clean, while the sister, at that time four, was still soiling herself. In school the patient was bright, while her sister was dull. The sister was heavy-set, therefore the patient wanted to be just the opposite. She said: "As long as my sister was present I was not allowed to be an individual". After her sister married, she tried unconsciously to make her brother-in-law admire her and did succeed in making him very fond of her. At times he even compared her with his wife to the patient's advantage. Once, when she noticed he was sexually attracted to her, she became at once panicky and enraged at him. She understood the situation, since she herself had become aware that her brother-in-law behaved in many respects just like her father. He was boastful and pretended to be a person of importance. She saw clearly that both the rage and panic really related primarily to her father. That insight enabled her to be more tolerant of her sister.

The same jealousy and competitiveness were present in relationship to her brother, but here there was also a protective motherly attitude. She remembered her visit to the hospital to see her brother who was born when she was five years old. Her parents were very happy to have a boy, but she declared that he looked like a little animal. During adolescence her brother used to tease her by singing a song he made up: "You are wrong, you are an accident", which she thought he must have heard from their parents. She was resentful because she felt that both brother and sister had nice names but that her name was ugly. She stated that it was unfortunate that as a baby she was not able to talk and object to her name. She identified herself very definitely with her brother when he was severely punished by father, for those occasions were proof to her that father did not love any of the children; then she felt justified in hating him.

In discussions of sexual matters she was shy and resentful. During the second year of analysis she fell in love with a young man whom she decided to marry after a few weeks of courtship. Then she talked of sexual matters more freely. Prior to that time, she talked about her love for children and the wish to have them, but she preferred that they be "test-tube" babies. During this courtship she enjoyed intimate contact with a man for the first time. It was also the first time she could admit her hunger for affection from a man and desire for dependence.

For some years she had been aware of desiring contact with men, although it usually happened when she felt depressed, miserable, and alone. She then engaged in petting parties, mostly because they enabled her to be close to someone. She also wanted to be nice to the men who desired petting, as if to repay them for the attention she thus secured. She feared that if she dressed attractively men would become attached to her. It gave her a peculiar pride to joke about her body which attracted men and to refer to her breasts as "hand-made" by petting.

It was apparent that her seeming ignorance about sexual matters was entirely the result of deep repression. As a matter of fact she knew a great deal about them and had experienced genital sensations. However, she rejected the knowledge in order not to be disturbed by it. She repeatedly expressed the desire to be sexless and when her father spoke cheerfully about her getting married, she wondered why he thought she would be happy, because she knew her parents' union was unhappy and that they never had had any affection for each other. Her fear of being hurt in coitus and in childbirth added to her conflicts about marrying: Being together with her fiancé so often, made her continually aware of being a woman. She thought that was bad for her because she feared losing control of herself. She was afraid to let him know she desired him. Because she desired constant affection she was terrified of the possibility of losing it. She described her need for love as a hunger. Her fantasies revealed its relationship to hunger for food. During her engagement she indulged more freely in loving and being loved and permitted herself passionate feelings. Nevertheless, she was seized by fear whenever her wedding plans were discussed because she felt that marriage would deprive her of her independence.

During this period she often spoke of her fiancé

as the ideal, capable, independent man of the world. She was horrified by the thought of his taking money from her father. Yet if they were to marry and live in the city it would be necessary to accept financial aid from him. Faced with this circumstance, her love turned to boundless hatred. Again her father would exercise his power over her with money. She therefore decided not to marry. She recognized, too, that since her love was an attempt to solve her problems "in flight" it would not be permanent. Her reaction to this situation once again brought the strong conflicts about father into the foreground. She cancelled her marriage plans, became depressed, cried almost continually for a few days, feeling as though she could never be happy. However, she did not have any eating difficulties. When the upset was over she began to feel more at ease at home. She understood more clearly at this time the emotional factors which caused her to be sick and she tried to carry out certain of her plans. For instance she had long cherished a wish to go back to school. Fear that she would not be able to remain there had caused her much unhappiness. She registered for several courses at college, and though her first visit to the registrar's office was a trying experience, because she felt like running out and crying, she stuck it out, and thereafter all went well. She enjoyed the courses and even made friends with some of the girls. She became aware once again of her attractiveness to men and began to enjoy their companionship even though her fear of attachment to them persisted. Going out with men still created problems for her. She was disturbed when anticipating dining out with them. At frequent intervals menstrual-like pains even though she had just menstruated, would occur. She recognized quite clearly, however, that on such occasions all these symptoms related to sex.

Through analysis of her dreams at this period, the fundamental points in her development were made understandable to her. All the dreams cited below occurred in the second year of analysis. Before that she did not take the trouble to remember dreams. She thought they were silly. If she did tell one occasionally she refused to discuss it and rejected any interpretation from the analyst. By the second year she came to understand the reasons for her fears and symptoms, hence she dared to face more of her fantasies and feelings and was more willing to remember and discuss her dreams. Through the understanding she derived from them she gained in ability to handle her problems. The following dreams show her attachment to her father, fear of him and concern about him.

"I was giving father his slippers". The same night she also dreamed: "I saw father stepping out of a car with a blonde girl".

The associations to these dreams brought out her resentment towards her father, her thoughts about the married life of her parents, and father's unhappiness. She also discussed the possibility that the mother caused the father's unhappiness at home, thereby forcing him to find solace in business and possibly in the company of other women. Some of her distrust of men was based on these thoughts about her father. She also understood that he did not like her because she nagged him as did her mother. The significance of giving the slippers to him was obvious even to her. It expressed her deep jealousy of mother, competition with her for father's affection, and her desire to keep him home and make him comfortable. This the patient often tried to do by preparing his favorite dishes and he would praise her for her efforts.

There were frequent dreams about babies. She was consciously fond of them and desired to have them but fear and guilt prevented her from freely indulging in such fantasies. The following dreams deal with this problem:

"Two babies are brought to our house. Two more beds were put in my room. The little baby was like a puppy. His feet were not like feet, his walk not like a walk, and his hands not like hands. There was a big dog chasing everybody".

In connection with this dream all her unhappiness concerning sibling rivalry came to the fore. The first signs of improvement in analysis came after her parents moved to a new apartment in which she was given her own room, no longer having to sleep with her sister. Sharing a room with her sister and having mother constantly entering the room, created many bitter hours for the patient. In the dream she repeats her conscious memories about the youngest child who appeared to her like a little animal when he was new-born; she also assures herself of superiority to this baby. The big dog chasing everybody in the dream referred to father, whom she many times thought of as a dog, and also to men in general. It also expressed fear of sexual approaches by men.

The anxieties concerning sexual involvements had their deepest roots in the strong desire to have a baby, a desire which was accompanied by fear and guilt because of her attachment to father and feeling of rivalry with mother. The following dream illustrates this problem:

"I am driving with father in a car. He had an accident. I asked him not to drive wildly. Then I got out of the car and met many girls from the school, but I had to get back into the car. I was reluctant. I was afraid".

She started her associations by stating: "I was an accident. Too bad that my parents had to have more children after my birth". Her father actually was a careless driver but never had an accident. Often when they rode together she was embarrassed because she did not know what to say to him, and he apparently reacted to her in the same way. She understood the sexual significance of the dream and said that she feared riding with men because they wanted to put their hands all over her; yet at times she encouraged advances, only to repel them once they were started. In the dream there was also an attempt to return to school, play with girls, and avoid the danger of growing up and facing sex. She was reluctant, but finally did step into the car. That was actually a reflection of her conscious attitude at the time. She had become more willing to accept the feminine role.

As she made greater attempts to adjust herself to the corrected ideas about sex, anxiety dreams dealing with sexual matters became more frequent. One of them is of special importance because it occurred in a menstrual period which was preceded by abdominal pains of a week's duration. (At the time of the dream her menses had been appearing regularly for several months. Prior to that she had amenorrhea.)

"The maid servant had a fur hat, and suddenly there appeared little leopards in the fur. There were many women in the room and all had leopards. I took one in my arms. It bit me. None of the women was bitten".

In her associations she talked about her earlier disgust with pubic hair. At puberty she tried to pull it out but was proud of the upper half of her body, especially the breasts, which she accentuated by her clothes. She had always suffered severe physical pain when her period was due, even when the menses did not appear. Not menstruating made her feel like an "it", she said. Yet she always had a dreadful apprehension of menstruation. She fantasied exploding with blood gushing out all over her, leaving her lifeless. On the other hand, she feared that if she did not menstruate she might explode. She expressed the conflict by saying "I want to bleed in order not to explode, but I am afraid to bleed because of the fact that all the blood will flow away".

She expressed the wish to be like other women and to have sexual intercourse, but at the same time she feared being "bitten". Being bitten referred to her childhood fantasies about castration which made her reject the lower part of her body as unattractive and "freakish".

She related the following dream:

"I am in the woods, little nude people, cannibals, savages, are all around.   I climb a tree".

She started her associations with something she was really reluctant to discuss.   Months before, during the summer on the beach, she accidentally saw the penis of one of her friends.   She was disgusted even when talking about it later.   It looked red, like a chunk of raw meat, she said.   The observation of the penis made her feel "gypped" as she did in childhood when she bought prize packages even though she knew she would be fooled.   "How", she asked, "can women be attracted to men when they know they will be cheated?"   Then she talked about eunuchs and hermaphrodites, sexual anomalies about which she had recently read.   At times she felt like a cannibal herself, having a desire to strangle the penis and yank it out.   She felt that way particularly after being passionate during petting.   At this time her petting was quite extensive, everything short of sexual intercourse, but becoming so passionate frightened her.   In other words, the cannibals in the dream represented men and penises, also her own savage desires.

In the course of that hour she complained about diarrhea when going out on a date and was embarrassed to have to discuss it with me.   She was surprised by this symptom which she could not remember ever having experienced before; as a rule she was constipated.

The sudden change from constipation to diarrhea was a last attempt to prevent herself from going out with men. Just a few days before she had proudly announced: "Do you want to know how much better I am? I have a blind date". Although she hated to go out, she had no disturbance before the date and ate her dinner. She chose where and how to go, and was hungry enough to eat again with the man later on in the evening. It seems as though she could no longer use oral symptoms as an excuse for not going out and so unconsciously used the diarrhea as an attempt to escape. On a deeper level this symptom signified masculine strivings. Her urinary frequency expressed the same masculine strivings and in addition masturbatory tendencies were expressed in diarrhea and urination, giving her an excuse to be pre-occupied with her genitals which she previously tried to disown.

To illustrate the general improvement, two additional dreams are cited which also clarify the psychodynamics of her symptoms. One day while commenting that the hair on her face and thighs was thinning out, she suddenly remembered a recent dream:

"An old man is doing electrolysis on my face. I was afraid it would leave scars, we were in mother's bedroom in the old house. He removed a few hairs".

Starting her associations, she mentioned that when she wakened that morning she looked in the mirror, saw that she had gained weight and suddenly thought: "Could I be pregnant? Could going out so many times and indulging in petting have caused me to become pregnant?" Then she remembered that at thirteen, while in the country she was frightened by a pregnant woman who told her that good country air helps women become pregnant. The old man in the dream was a friend of the family. She considered him a stingy pest because he always objected to giving his children anything. On the dream night, at a card-game at home her sister lost to father and when the sister's husband wanted to pay the loss, father insisted the money be paid by sister. He enjoyed making her pay because she was stingy. The patient in associating then continued, "I am glad sister cannot have a baby. I am mean, I know, but if someone has to have a baby, I want to have it". In the light of this remark the whole dream was understandable. The electrolysis performed in mother's bedroom really referred to her primary wish in the Œdipus situation. Hair is masculine, she wanted to be made a woman by father in mother's bed and have a baby by him. Her fear of scars refers to the fear of permanent punishment which would accompany gratification of these guilt-charged desires.

The next dream is of importance because it shows the extent of her improvement in the transference relationship:

"I had an appointment at twelve for my analytic hour. I forgot it, and it was late. I called your office and you said it does not matter because you were going fishing. Your voice was faint and getting weaker and weaker. You told me that you were poisoned. I wanted to tell you to be careful, that you must live, instead of which I said, 'be careful, M. must live'. (M. was the name by which the patient was called when she was a child, later it was changed.) Then you ceased to talk and I felt panicky. I looked for a telephone number to call your home".

Then she remembered that there was an additional part with which the dream started:

"You told me you have broad shoulders and you do not like it.   I reassured you that I do like it. Then you asked me whether I think of men these days, and I said, I do, and I also think about you".

Her associations to this dream brought out the many thoughts and feelings which she had about analysis and analysts in general; her criticism and scorn in the past, but how later she learned to trust the method of treatment because she was handled with patience and kindness.   She was exceedingly embarrassed to report the part of the dream in which she felt that the analyst must live, because it was an admission of identification of the analyst with the kind of father she would have liked to have.   That is also why she called herself "M", a name which she used only until the age of fourteen.   The analyst's being poisoned brought up ideas about his unfaithfulness and consequent contraction of some disease.   This led directly to her ideas about pregnancy, which was equated in her unconscious with being poisoned. Further associations referred to her feeling that her life was poisoned by her father's constant watching and disapproval of her.   The first part of the dream which was remembered later, clearly shows her attachment to and her preoccupation with the analyst.   At that stage of analysis she was ready to acknowledge it. She also referred to vaginal sensations other than pain, at times rather vague, at others definitely pleasurable. She mentioned that when dancing she was aware of genital sensations and a slight vaginal discharge.

The above dream occurred after a little more than two years of analysis. By that time her anorexia and amenorrhea had been completely cured and the psychodynamics of her neurosis became clear in all their ramifications. In her case all the disturbances seem to have had as their primary cause the reactions to the mother's attitude from earliest infancy. The whole symptom complex centered around the problem of how to deal with her and later with the indifferent father as well. They were the two people who made her, as she termed it, "starve".

She remembers that in early childhood she was like a little beast who wanted to eat up and tear up everything and everyone. Her jealousies started with sibling rivalry at the early age of two. At this age her father became linked with her oral cravings and from then on these desires carried sexual charges.

The eating disturbances were connected with an unconscious concept of the poisonous content of food and this idea related to fantasies of oral impregnation. Thus the ideas were formulated that food was dangerous just as intercourse and pregnancy were. Early, confusing experiences in relation to food and love caused hostility and consequent guilt feelings which she tried to expiate with intense masochism. In depressed phases she had suicidal impulses and strong wishes to die. When unable to eat and miserable with abdominal pains she consoled herself by repeating: "It wont last long, tomorrow I will die". In her deepest unconscious the inability to eat expressed her wish to waste away and die. Self-punishment tendencies were an outstanding part of her symptoms. She recognized them as representing simultaneous punishment of her parents as well. They wanted love when she no longer could give it. Instead she showed resentment and caused worry. Her symptoms were also an attempt to win affection. For in her illness she had become the center of anxious attention as never before.

The analysis proved without question that the oral symptom (her reaction to food) served to realize other fantasies which were of primary importance to the patient. In a symbolic way eating was equated with sexuality. All symptoms centering around eating could be transposed to her problems of sexuality. In the deepest layer there was the primary desire for impregnation, to become fat, to have a big abdomen. The guilt associated with that desire resulted in the expression of the opposite, namely a denial by expulsion, or vomiting out the stomach content, all of which also indicated her belief that there was danger in "getting fat". The fantasy of oral impregnation was clearly proven in the course of analysis, when she used nausea and loss of appetite to avoid engagements with men. The fear of being poisoned by food also expressed the fear of pregnancy but at the same time it concealed hostility towards her parents, feelings which she expressed by vomiting. It was retaliation for their "poisoning" of her life.

The disturbance of bowel function, constipation, was in the service of the same unconscious fantasies. While the oral symptoms meant intake and conception, constipation realized the wish of permanent impregnation. The intestinal tract was definitely symbolic to her of the womb, and functioned like it in some respects.

The jealousy which started with feeding became attached to the problem of sibling favoritism. In this way it also became connected with love and sex. She was precocious in childhood, but genital sexuality had become repulsive to her because of the whole early childhood Œdipus involvement. Unconsciously she had good reason to reject all men and sex. In analysis she realized that she really had no aversion to them, but only to marriage. That was the problem against which she had to protect herself because of the implication of pregnancy and also because of her observations of the unhappy marital life of her parents. She also had to reject genitality because of her fear of being exposed; she considered herself abnormal because from early childhood on she had always had some ailment. This she later connected with ideas about sexual disorders. With the onset of menstrual disturbances she became convinced that there was something wrong with her sexually. Amenorrhea expressed denial of femininity. The fear of exploding when not menstruating was derived from guilt and the fear of being pregnant, giving birth, being injured, and dying. The object of amenorrhea was to conceal abnormality which being a woman meant to her unconsciously.

Her social and sexual passivity was a continuation of infantile passivity resulting from early fears and which later served as a defense. Her feeling that she was an unwanted child was the root of her fundamental distrust of everyone and everything. This I consider a very important factor in her case.

The symptoms were all elaboration and acting out of emotions which were bound up with infantile and childhood experiences. Feelings concerning mother, father, sister, brother, and representatives of the outside world effected disturbances in the gastro-intestinal tract. Emotional reactions to people which could not be verbalized sought expression through the same channels which were employed for this purpose in early childhood. All the bitterness and pain relating to the earliest disappointments by mother and which were primarily bound up with feeding, care, and affection, remained the source of her permanent distrust of everybody. "If I cannot trust mother or father, how can I trust anyone?" She tried to utilize, in the solution of her emotional conflicts, organs which were particularly sensitive to psychic stimuli. Her whole gastro-intestinal tract, to which system (in her unconscious) the whole abdominal content belonged, was used to express and to reject cravings, including pregnancy and the defense against it. It also served to express love and hate in the same manner that every child, in the course of early development, uses excretion and the intake of food as means of expressing love, obedience, rejection, and hate.

When all conversion symptoms, vomiting, abdominal pain, disgust with food, menstrual difficulties, had disappeared and the patient's general, social attitude and attitude toward sex changed considerably, the basic problem, her moodiness and depression, still created difficulties for which she continued treatment another two years. The oral problems which were so prominent in her hysterical symptoms and which related to her mother were also responsible for her depression. Of outstanding importance were: first, the feeling of being unwanted, especially by mother; second, the severe superego, which was a result of the inverted aspects of infantile aggression; third, the difficulty in identification with mother and the consequent weak ego structure.

Being freed of her eating difficulties and developing more maturity in social relations, her attitude towards men became healthier, but still analytic hours were spent in crying and complaining about the impossibility of going on. This time all her complaints were connected with sexual feelings, strong desires of finding someone, marrying, and having children. But at the same time she was as yet unable to accept completely the strong sexual urges because they always carried feelings of frustration, depression, and a renewed sense of not belonging.

It was difficult for her to develop a transference relationship in the first period of her analysis, but in this period her dependence, attachment, sexual feelings, and need for love came forth with elementary force. Nothing could satisfy her clamoring for affection and as a result she felt frustrated and depressed for about a month.

The wealth of material gained in the first part of her

analysis and during the month of her depression
afforded the opportunity of observing the important
role the early fixation played in her neurosis. Rather
complicated mechanisms behind her depression all
pointed to emotional disturbances in the relationship
to her mother. Her deep-rooted insecurity which is
so prominent a feature in depression was connected
with the early oral and anal fixations and their
frustrations.

In the transference relationship her feeling of need
for security became very real in contrast to the previous period when she felt self-sufficient and independent, superficially, of course. Behind this seeming
independence was her constant fear of forming emotional attachments and being frustrated as she had
been in childhood. The analyst's person became the
desired object of her instinctual strivings which had
never been satisfied. The forgotten pregenital and
Œdipus fixations of childhood emerged in the transference relationship and were projected with all the
early strong demands upon the analyst. The patient
described fantasies of clinging to him and in the next
moment pushing him away. Dreams of sexual intercourse with the analyst, fondling him and being
fondled, were of frequent occurrence. She fantasied
complete happiness and relaxation in the act of sexual
union with the analyst. Her defenses of keeping her
sexual feelings and reactions on an infantile level,
which had been present throughout the first part of
her analysis, were completely broken down.

Through externalizing sexual feelings and need for
dependence in the analytical situation, she learned to

be less afraid and to accept feminine sexual feeling in the highest degree. A new type of self-recognition began to develop which enabled her to know and appreciate herself fundamentally as a woman. Reorganization of her genital functioning also began as a result of externalization of feelings in analysis and the pre-genital trends, which previously were outstanding in her behavior to men, slowly began to be absorbed by a more normal sexual attitude. She reached the point of being willing, at least in the transference relationship, to give up her defenses and to realize all her repressed instinctual drives. She was willing to abandon her substitute forms of sexual gratification if the analyst would satisfy her desires. Sexual feelings no longer frightened her so much and she had fewer conflicts about them. This was a type of ego-strength different from the earlier, constant fear of the superego. She began to be able to tolerate sexual feelings and accompanying fantasies to a degree she never had expected to achieve.

Such a strong transference relationship as this patient developed because of her early desires and their complete frustration, may make the patient wish to cling to analysis and be unwilling to renounce this relationship. This is the usual drawback in depressions and other borderline cases. A very strong object relationship is created because it is the first time that the patient has been permitted to experience real attachment. The patient may not want to curb it or give it up because of the opportunity it provides to discharge emotions heretofore forcibly repressed. The projection onto the analyst of early childhood feelings will be indulged in to extremes. But, by tireless, patient working through, the patient learns to differentiate between what is *past* and what belongs to the *present* and learns to cope with such impulses on a reality basis.

Since the transference desires aroused sexual excitement, the depressive anxieties became more prominent because frustration by the analyst reinforced the primary anxieties of the past which were caused by her mother's frustrating attitude. In addition, this early frustration by mother made the patient seek more dependence and tenderness from father in her early childhood. But these Œdipus attachments were shattered and in the analytical transference the entire experience with father was repeated, thus aggravating the patient's depression. At times she appeared unable to endure the strain which those conflicting and shifting emotions created. Her disappointment in not having her sexual desires gratified goaded her on to express her aggressive feelings but they were accompanied by a sense of guilt, and fear of punishment by the analyst. Abusive language was indulged in, first with some restraint, then more freely, but all the while she felt extremely depressed. Every day she left the analytical hour with the idea of not returning. During this period of frustration she believed that the analyst had become severe, as her parents always were in reality and she reacted by being depressed just as she had done in childhood.

In the first part of her analysis, the analyst's aim was to eliminate her feelings of being unwanted. In the second period she herself demanded continued proof of being wanted. The first part of analysis effected a change in her attitude towards her parents; she learned to trust them and hence her aggression and guilt were reduced, with the result that she was less terrified of reality. In the second part of treatment the analytical process was an incessant battle in which the patient went through all the periods of adaptation that she had skipped in childhood.

She had to learn to tolerate frustrations as they arose in the course of analysis. These frustrations, which she felt keenly, were mainly a repetition of the traumatic frustrations and fears of her earliest relationship to her mother. This was why her anxiety was overwhelming and why, as soon as one fear was dispelled, a new panic sprang up to replace it. Her earliest memory was that of being wheeled around in a baby carriage, in connection with which period her mother told her she was so ugly that she was ashamed to show her to other people. Such traumatic occurrences in infancy created a fertile soil on which her adult depression developed. The tendency to self-abasement, and self-reproach, her inhibitions, her sadness, her constant complaints of mental inadequacy all resulted from these early experiences. Re-experiencing these feelings and tendencies so strongly in the analytical situation brought out the tremendous aggression with which they were bound up. The feeling of being unwanted and the conflicts which developed as a result, involved not only the mother; from the mother it was transposed to all members of the family. Mother's frustrating, threatening, punishing attitude stood out conspicuously in the patient's recollection. It overshadowed all the tenderness and love her mother may have shown her. Later the siblings and father made her feel the same: unwanted and unloved. And so the aggression which she showed in relation to the analyst and the whole world, had to be redirected to her environment: mother, father, and siblings. The extreme ambivalence also was shown in her alternating feelings of aggression and self-depreciation. After an aggressive phase, she usually tried to show how worthless she was and would say that the time spent on her treatment should be given to cure someone else. In addition to self-punishment, this attitude also served the purpose of assuring pity and help.

To bring her to more mature feelings and to full recognition of the fact that her behavior in analysis was a repitition of early childhood experiences, was a very slow process. The guidance and educational influences which were effective in the first part of her analysis were not of much use in this period. This time the frustration of her wish to be loved by the analyst made her feel depressed and beaten; to bear this frustration was an extraordinary hardship for her. During the first part of her analysis, when constant vomiting made her weak and miserable, she had to be given a type of treatment that Ferenczi described as "child analysis with adults". I encouraged her to come even when she felt very weak and sick. I induced her mother to send her to my office in a taxi cab. In the early months of her analysis, I changed appointments according to her inconsequential personal program. If she wanted to change an analytic hour in order to go shopping, I complied with her wishes. Occasionally I administered different kinds of medication: prescribed for a cold or bandaged a cut finger.

The home environment was controlled as much as it was possible to do: I instructed the mother about her attitude towards the patient, induced her to move to a larger apartment in which the patient could have her own room and persuaded her to consent to the patient's decorating the room herself. The mother was also instructed not to go into the patient's room unless invited. During the analytical hour the patient sometimes lay on the couch, sometimes sat in a chair or paced the floor excitedly. When she had progressed sufficiently in treatment, she was advised to go back to college which became a source of great pleasure for her. After a while she enrolled for a shorthand and typing course, upon the completion of which she secured a position. When she tired of one job, she was encouraged to change it, and did. When in doubt as to whether to go away for a weekend or remain at home, I decided for her by pointing out that she could always return if she was not enjoying herself.

This type of handling of insecure, infantile behavior is not unique or even rare. Many analysts, I am sure, have had the opportunity to help patients through extremely difficult phases by means of such elastic techniques. In this particular patient's case I believe that it would not have been possible to cure her in any other way.

Other techniques had to be used during the period of her depression. The first step, as in all depressions, was to reduce the negative attitude and to bring about a positive transference. Once the positive transference has been established, it must be strengthened. Because of the fundamental distrust these patients feel, the analyst will have to exert new efforts in that direction daily. Generally, in depression, it is inadvisable to analyze the transference at an early period, for when the patient is negative, interpretation is of no avail. In this case, however, due to the preceding period of analysis, the transference was analyzed whenever it became apparent. But as for her actions, sometimes I had to wait quite a while before the patient was in a frame of mind in which she was able to understand and accept interpretations of them.

During these periods of negative behavior, the externalization of her aggressive feelings helped in reducing her feelings of guilt in connection with her thoughts, speech, and acts. In this manner her ego was strengthened, and she learned to accept impulses previously forbidden by her superego. The externalization of aggression decidedly aided in the reduction of the severity of her superego. Tolerance and patience during the periods when her aggressive feelings came to the fore, gave the patient the feeling that she was getting sympathy even though the analyst's behavior did not completely satisfy her craving for love. Bringing her to realize that the analyst was undisturbed by the different emotional reactions to which he was exposed helped a great deal in the reorganization of her feelings about early childhood frustrations. In spite of her accusations when going through painful periods, she became conscious of the sincere efforts of the analyst. This was what always brought her back in spite of daily threats of not returning. Working through her relationship to the analyst, slowly brought the realization that her childhood experiences had not been just traumatic but that they had also sometimes been pleasant. In analysis she experienced a different kind of relationship to the superego than that to which she had been accustomed from childhood on. The frustrated, threatening, and punishing attitude which stood out most conspicuously in the patient's recollection of her superego (parents) was changed through experiencing a different type of superego (analyst). Effective interpretation and continually working through the early patterns, comparing the patient's reactions in early childhood with her reactions to current reality situations, helped also to dispel her early impressions and anxieties, together with the tendency to escape reality.

The usual rules for analysis do not suffice in depression. The complete lack of stability of the ego in these cases makes for extreme, aggressive tendencies. During the course of treatment the analyst frequently meets with discouragement: for each step forward the patient may seem to slip back two. But the analyst must always keep alert, have inexhaustible patience, and be prepared for a tedious, time-consuming process. It is important for the therapeutic results that there should be somebody in the family to whom the patient feels attached, someone by whom he feels accepted. It is my opinion that depressed patients whose parents are dead present a more difficult problem for therapy than those, both or one of whose parents is alive, not only because of the object-love present, but also because the patient's death-wishes against the parents do not find realization in his mind if the parents are still alive. When they are dead, the guilt feelings connected with death wishes against them are very strong because of the patient's unconscious belief that his wishes may have caused their death. The hostility which these patients have against their parents cannot be redirected to the original source.

After one has made certain that the patient is on the road to improvement and that analysis has resulted in a better adjustment, the treatment may still go on for a long time during which the object relationships which the patient begins to develop have to be strengthened and encouraged. This is the period when the patient's actions and behavior, which he could not fully understand or appreciate in the depressive phase, are analyzed and worked through. It is not difficult to determine when this period of improvement has become stable and progressive, for the patient's suicidal thoughts hardly appear, all delusions are gone, and more neurotic symptoms, especially obsessions, come to the fore.

The degree of adjustment after analysis in cases of depressive states depends upon the degree of stability of the ego. A high degree of plasticity and elasticity in the ego means a low degree of stability. In such cases patients are likely to show extreme regressive tendencies, hence their adjustment after analysis is less satisfactory. If a certain amount of rigidity is present in the patient's character, it indicates strength in the ego and therefore the results of psychoanalytic treatment are more promising. It is this ego strength, therefore, which is responsible for varying degrees of severity in cases of depression. The same factors are at work in all depressive states, but widely divergent quantitative emotional disturbances appear in various patients in direct proportion to the ego strength or lack of it.

Chapter IX

DREAM ANALYSIS

Dream interpretation has a fascination for beginning analysts, many of whom show great enthusiasm for their patients' dreams. Enthusiasm, however, is not sufficient to produce good results. The ability to interpret dreams depends upon many factors of which experience, based on knowledge of the origin and structure of dreams, is the most important. The analyst's aptitude, personality, and intuition are also of importance, but only in combination with specific knowledge of the nature of dreams.

Freud's discovery of the meaning of dreams has been the greatest contribution to our knowledge of the structure of the mind. Dream analysis is of primary importance in psychoanalytic therapy as dreams are the via regia to the unconscious.

Freud attributed the origin of the dream to two conflicting tendencies: one, the desire for sleep, second, the tendency to satisfy a mental stimulus. Its function, as Freud pointed out, is to protect sleep and the two main characteristics are wish-fulfillment and hallucinatory experience.

In therapy, the latent meaning of the dream must be reconstructed from the manifest content. The technique of dream interpretation has its fundamental rules but it is essentially an art, as are other elements of psychoanalytic technique. Through experience each therapist develops his individual approach. The basic rule which must be adhered to is to use the patient's free associations to the manifest content. The analyst must not attempt to translate the dream solely on the basis of his own associations to it, or his concept of the meaning of its symbols. Those who have had only limited experience in psychoanalysis are prone to interpret through dream symbolism exclusively.

There are individual variations in the manner and degree of exploitation of symbols and in the approach to interpretation in general. Some analysts begin by investigating the role of current events in activating the dreams and then follow up with the patient's associations. Others interpret only through the patient's associations. One may have a flair for special types of dreams and be inclined to analyze and thoroughly exploit the latent content of these, but give short translation-like interpretations of others, with attention focussed on the manifest dream wishes rather than on the latent content.

One of the physicians being supervised by me, presented the following dream brought in by one of his patients:

"My friend M. (a sickly young man) is crossing the street. He has on a hat and he is smiling."

His patient's associations brought out the following main ideas: M. (the friend) is constantly cared for by his mother, even to the extent that she knows of the prostitutes who visit him and encourages him to receive them. Everyone in M.'s home is subservient to him because of his illness. In contrast, the patient is always made to feel at fault by the constant criticism of all the members of his family, especially his mother. His main symptoms are exhibitionism, voyeurism, and impotence. Other associations of the patient concern arguments in his home a few days earlier which led him to compare himself with M., noting how much better off his friend was.

On the basis of the associations, the dream seemed to me to indicate the following: M. is carelessly crossing the street, happy, unconcerned about the onrushing traffic. He is behaving like a carefree child, whom everyone has to help and give attention. He can do no wrong. The traffic on the streets must stop when he crosses. He can expose himself (exhibit his sexuality) without shame or fear, like a happy child. Having his hat on and smiling referred to the patient's wish to exhibit his penis, and his enjoyment of the activity. Throughout this dream the patient identifies himself with his friend, M. who is so happy and carefree, whose mother gives him every attention, and who can exhibit his sexuality without fear.

After the dream had been interpreted for the analyst in the control hour, he later presented it at a seminar on dreams led by another training analyst, who explained it differently. This colleague emphasized the homosexual component. According to his interpretation the dream expressed the patient's homosexuality: M. is a woman with a penis, and crossing the street smilingly means he is a prostitute. The student claimed that the seminar leader rejected all other approaches or explanations. Such rigidity is always a mistake. Although these two interpretations differ widely, both have validity and may describe the content of the patient's unconscious. His being sexually impotent and a voyeur, unquestionably is connected with unconscious homosexual and feminine tendencies. However, his associations to this particular dream did not touch upon those tendencies.

The foregoing illustrates what is meant by a flair for a particular mode of interpretation. The same preference or prejudice is possible with regard to the handling of dream symbols. Some analysts tend to interpret symbols with absolute certainty and to concentrate upon one meaning of the symbol. True, a number of symbols are considered to have universal significance, but others can only be understood through the patient's associations. The latter type, if "translated" and interpreted by the analyst without the patient's associations, may provoke justified contradiction and even be flatly rejected by the patient. In those cases only the associations of the patient will illuminate the import of the symbol and give an acceptable meaning to the dream itself.

The problem of the symbolic meaning of the mantle will serve as an example. According to Jones [1] the mantle symbolizes the penis. As proof of his interpretation he points out that the mantle is an easily detachable part of a person's clothing and that there is a similarity between the ease with which the arms slip in and out of an overcoat, and the mobility of the skin covering the penis. It would be rather difficult to make the patient understand and accept the validity of such an interpretation unless it can be explained and supported with more definite associations.

[1] The Mantle Symbol, *Int. J. Psa.* Vol. VIII, 1927.

As a result of a chain of associations to two dreams of a female patient, I elaborated upon Jones' interpretation.[2] In her associations she connected the mantle which covers one's body with the original body covering, hair; and to the hair she associated the hairy body, which signified masculinity to her. The two dreams were as follows:

"I am going to take a bath with a woman friend. I am wearing a bathrobe of Mr. X (her lover) which he used to put on when he undressed for intercourse. I wear the coat in order not to catch cold".

"I am passing by a butcher's shop where I buy my meat. The butcher is standing in the doorway and looks sad when he sees me carrying a basket containing a turkey. I go in to buy another turkey, but on the hooks around the wall where the meat usually hangs, there are fur coats".

She started the train of associations by saying that she was excited sexually and was "out for *scalps* again". Then she talked about liking to playfully pull the hair on a man's body, particularly the hair on the chest. She continued with the following associations: a hairy body signifies masculinity, a cave man. Her lover is bald; his body is not hairy either; he does not satisfy her sexually. In the dream she has the coat in order not to catch cold, not to be left cold by her lover who is bald (not masculine). She herself has the penis (robe-mantle) and plays the role of a man.

In the second dream fur coats replace meat; meat represents a penis to her; fur coats also represent masculinity (penises). The butcher is a masculine, hairy caveman but she disappoints him, makes him sad because she has her own penis (turkey in the basket). Thus she arrived at the interpretation of the coat (mantle) being a penis, by a chain of associations from the coat to the hair on the body and from there to a description of all the men who "fell" for her when she was out "collecting scalps", (which really meant her wish to collect penises). To have simply told this patient that the coat meant a penis would have eliminated her affirmative associations.

As another example let us consider the symbol of vermin or lice, which usually is interpreted as representing children. A female patient had the following dream after having had pediculosis pubis which she successfully exterminated:

"I had lice in my head; nice, big ones. Something is growing on my body and I am nursing it of my own flesh and blood".

In her associations she talked about the following: her resentment towards men and penises, her desire to exterminate men. She would like to have nails growing around her genital region in order to hurt men during intercourse. The "something growing" on her body she interpreted as being her own penis. The usually accepted meaning of vermin as the symbol of babies, was not even hinted at in her associations. However, it could also have been interpreted as such because of material previously presented concerning the wish for a baby.

One can only become skilled in the art of dream

interpretation through experience, and the beginning analyst will do well to refrain from being hasty in trying to understand all that the language of the dream conveys. A symbol may be universal, but the patient can have his own way of presenting what the symbol usually stands for. One may say that the cat is a symbol for the female, but then the patient, in associations, leads to an interpretation in which the cat in that particular dream is a tomcat and hence stands for a male. The patient's associations and interpretations must be respected. It will be found especially necessary to credit them in cases where the patient usually refuses to give any associative material and the analyst is forced to interpret the dreams on the basis of his previously acquired knowledge of the person's unconscious tendencies. After the analyst has interpreted, the patient is usually ready to give his ideas. Naturally his object will be to prove the analyst wrong, and it may happen that the patient's interpretation is the correct one.

Very often, especially in character neuroses, the patient brings in extremely distorted dreams with few or no associations. No matter how many attempts the analyst makes to take the manifest content apart, no associations come forth. The next step is to try to interpret the dream on the basis of the symbolism used by the dreamer. These are the occasions which call for versatility on the part of the analyst and a knowledge of the language of symbolism. Even if the patient rejects the interpretation as far-fetched and nonsensical the therapist is compelled to make use of that type of explanation in order to penetrate more deeply into the latent content, because the main purpose of interpretation is to understand the dreamwork. The domain of symbolism is extensive and some knowledge of anthropology, mythology, folklore, art, and literature is essential to the understanding of the origin and usage of symbols.

It is important to make patients realize that their dreams have meaning, and to teach them to accept the dream as a product of their own mind. Therefore it is advisable to be cautious, and refrain from starting dream interpretation early in analysis. How long a period should elapse before dream interpretation is begun cannot be specified. But it is a good rule to wait until one knows a good deal about the patient's life and difficulties, especially the conflicts which have brought on his illness. However, this, too, cannot be strictly adhered to. A patient may have a severe panic early in analysis and a superficial interpretation of his dreams may make the meaning of his panic understandable to him, thereby helping him over the acute phase.

Before starting interpretation, I usually explain to the patient the origin and meaning of dreams. For a starting point I always use daydreams, which no patient refuses to recognize as his own productions, even if he labels them as silly and refuses to consider them. It is then not difficult for the patient to go a step further and be willing to admit some meaning to the dreams produced in his sleep. At this point I also explain the reason for dream distortion, showing how the *censor* creates that distortion in order to make the dream seem meaningless or absurd. Freud explained the problem of distortion as follows:

"The tendencies which exercise the censorship are those which are acknowledged by the waking judgment of the dreamer . . . . The dream censorship is directed against tendencies which are invariably of an objectionable nature, offensive from the ethical, aesthetic, or social point of view . . . . These censored wishes, which in dreams are expressed in a distorted fashion, are manifestations of boundless and ruthless egoism; for the dreamer's own Ego makes its appearance in every dream and plays the principal part, even if it knows how to disguise itself completely . . ."

The mechanism and function of distortion are clearly shown in the following dream of a female patient:

"I am with a group in the woods; cannibals come on huge horses. I realize we shall be eaten. I escape".

The outstanding feature of the dream was the absence of fright on the part of the patient. She spoke of the cannibals as being good-natured. The distortion was due to the latent dream thought, which dealt with the Œdipus situation: her direct wish for her father, which involved taking mother's place, and fear of this desire. Her associations led back to her concept of intercourse. The fear of being eaten was a symbolic expression of her fear of sexual intercourse. Being eaten was a displacement from below upwards and represented fear of being annihilated during the sexual act.

A young girl, struggling with sexual problems, had the following dream:

"I have a small leopard in my arms. It has long nails and I am afraid that it will scratch me. There is a group of women. I notice that they all have leopards, and they do not seem to be afraid".

The patient's acute problem at the time of this dream was the breaking through of her sexual desires which she had for years tried to deny, to the extent of not wanting to take cognizance of the lower part of her body, referring to her genital region jokingly as "no man's land". Her severe, painful amenorrhea had been corrected and her relationship to men began to be more positive, but the constant fear of sexuality, attachment to men and her distrust of them, were topics of daily discussion in analysis. The manifest dream was stimulated by her having bought a leopard muff and hat during the preceding few days. At its deepest level of meaning the dream referred to the dangers of having a vagina and being like other women.

Distortions which at times call for symbolic interpretation may be extensive, and are characteristic of certain types of patients. Special patterns of distortion are common in character neurosis.

It is extremely important to pay close attention to the affects which the patient experiences in his dreams. In the dream of the cannibals, just cited, the patient's feelings were not unpleasant. She described the cannibals as friendly. In the dream about leopards, the patient spoke about the fear of being scratched. The same girl dreamed the following, from which she awoke in a panic:

"A heavy man is on top of me".

Another dream of hers at the same period in analysis:

"A frog was in my bed". (Again she awoke in a panic.)

She related that after the latter dream she felt dazed for several minutes, then switched on the light and actually looked in her bed for a frog. At other times she had the same kind of dream with cockroaches and snakes and went through the procedure of looking for them when she awoke.

Usually there are no indications of feelings in dreams, or, if present, are milder than the patient's actual, repressed feeling associated with the unconscious, latent desires. When analyzing and interpreting such feelings, the therapist has the opportunity to convince the patient of their original intensity at the time they were repressed. The dream-work alters the feelings associated with the dream content, sometimes suppressing completely all feelings which would normally be present, sometimes converting them into their opposites, as, for instance, in the dream about the cannibals. Its most frequent effect is to reduce the intensity of the feelings.

If emotions are displayed in the manifest dream content, the patient accepts more readily the interpretation of the underlying desires, which results in his permitting further repressed material to come through. If the manifest dream seems flat and without signs of feeling, one is sure to find emotional charges in the latent dream content through the patient's associations.

Another of the many mechanisms utilized in dream work, is *condensation*. In the case of dreams that are short and apparently simple, one may be inclined to give a superficial interpretation or explanation, because in contrast to the average dream, they seem like short statements. The patient's dream of having a heavy man on top of her one might be inclined to accept solely for the manifest content: fear of being under a heavy man, fear of intercourse. However, her associations proved it to have a close relationship to the imagined *primal scene*. She thought of herself as a little girl; the heavy man represented her father whom she desired, yet feared. Her childhood ideas about the sex relationship were of an outstandingly sadistic nature because they were based on her observations of the hostile relationship between her parents.

The dream must be interpreted from many angles because of the variety of mechanisms utilized to disguise its meanings. *Secondary elaboration* is one of these mechanisms and is the chief factor in the creation of the manifest content. Whatever is intelligible in the manifest dream is, to an extent, a disguise and a distortion of the latent, repressed thoughts, another reason to beware of interpreting the manifest dream simply on the basis of symbolism.

The translation of symbols, through which the dream makes its manifest meaning known, is futile, because it is incomplete and usually not convincing to the patient. Even if the analyst has become gen-

erally acquainted with the patient's life and suspects
the wish behind the manifest dream, translation of
the symbols is about as effective as an explanation of
a symptom; in other words it effects no real change.

Constant awareness of the regressive tendencies of
the dream is another important factor in the technique
of interpretation. The object of the regressive trend
is to recall the early memory pictures. Even if there
is no definite sign of regression in the manifest dream,
the analyst's familiarity with the problems of the
patient, and his knowledge that all neurotic individuals
try to escape from reality are sufficient to enable him
to point out to the patient the inclination in the latent
context, to return to early childhood scenes.

For instance, a male patient, suffering from sexual
difficulties, had the following dream:

"I am in a men's toilet and I want to urinate. A
husky man stands near me and tries to push me and
crowd me out".

The patient did not notice any affect in the dream.
However, his associations brought out material concerning fear of rivalry, and he constantly reiterated
the query: "What is the use of trying"? which was an
expression of his desire to run away, avoid competition and be free of the obligation to try to improve
his environment.

This dream occurred in a period of his analysis
when he was actually making attempts to find a better
position; he took up more contacts in his profession,
made plans to get away from home and tried to be
more independent in every respect. The dream represented **the unconscious** wish for the opposite in order

to spare himself a repetition of difficulty and embarrassment which he had experienced in the past. It was as if his unconscious were saying, "You see, you are trying, you are exposing your penis and comparing it with the next man's; you may try to compete with him but he is stronger and can push you out. Better not try".

Another important function of the dream and its associated thoughts is that of providing an opportunity for the patient to recognize his asocial tendencies and selfish drives, factors in the latent content of the dream which hitherto he has refused to own. Dreams assist in bringing them to light and their examination leads to a deeper understanding of the source of the neurosis.

To analyze a dream in all its ramifications is hardly possible. Some dreams, however, can be analyzed to relative completion. To do so interpretation should be attempted from four different angles.

1. *The residue of the preceding day*. A particular event may have been the stimulus for the dream, in which case there is an opportunity to discuss the difference between the patient's reality situation and the wish expressed in the dream.

2. *The regressive tendency*. Every dream expresses in some form the patient's desire to adhere to old patterns of behavior rather than struggle to achieve a new adjustment. For instance, the dreams of impotent men and frigid women contain the wish to cling to childhood attitudes toward sex.

3. *The Œdipus relationship*. The discussion of the tendency to regress to childhood leads to an exami-

nation of the reaction patterns resulting from the patient's early attachment to parents.

4. *The analytical situation.* If the dream does not deal directly with the analysis, one can usually find evidence of thoughts and feelings concerning the treatment or the therapist in the events of the preceding day which have stimulated the dream. For the transference relationship repeatedly stirs feelings of affection, frustration, and hostility, which the patient often transposes to his other relationships and activities and these feelings thus become indirect stimuli of the dream.

In connection with the foregoing, the wish-fulfillment aim of every type of dream must be given its full evaluation, even in the painful, punishment-fulfillment dreams. The latter type of dream-wish seems paradoxical unless examined in relation to the patient's unconscious conflicts.

A young colleague once expressed to me his annoyance with one of his patients for continually repeating the same kind of dream, associative material, and behavior. Although all the material of the dream had been worked through, the same type appeared again and again during the eight months of analysis. I suggested that he continue interpreting the dreams, but to concentrate on the relationship of the dreams to reality and the patient's resistance to understanding their emotional context. Within a few weeks after the analyst had begun to work along these lines, the patient commenced to show a negativistic attitude in the transference relationship and the dreams reflected more aggression. Working through these newly expressed attitudes, connecting them with current reality and with childhood experiences, helped reduce the patient's resistance which had caused the stagnation of his analysis.

Changes in the nature of the dream provide a reliable clue to the patient's progress. If there is a reduction of anxiety and tension in the dreams for a considerable period and their content shows a more positive attitude, it can be taken as a favorable prognostic. Where there is a continuation of anxiety dreams that constantly emphasize escape attitudes and resistance to progress, it is an indication that in the deep strata of the unconscious analysis has not brought about sufficient change, even if externally the patient's behavior has improved to the extent of a reduction of symptoms.

The following dream indicated progress, even though at the time the patient, who had nymphomanic tendencies and the desire to castrate men, was not yet able to function satisfactorily.

"I see mother, cold and composed. She says: 'No use, you won't succeed with your sex' ".

Around the time of this dream she experienced excruciating abdominal pains whenever coitus was attempted. It was at a stage in her analysis when her main desire (in complete contrast to her previous wishes) was to have a child. She had more sexual feeling than ever before, but only in connection with fantasies. In the above dream, she at last confronts her mother, of whom we had talked for the preceding three years as being the main cause of her troubles, in that the aggression and guilt she had provoked in the patient precluded identification with her (the mother). In her associations to this dream she said that her vagina was "closed" because of her desire for a baby. In other words, she recognized the fact that she was still unable to accept full femininity (motherhood), because it would have equalled identification with her mother, whom she still hated.

Early in his analysis, a patient suffering from a compulsion neurosis had the following dream:

"I was with my friend, an officer. A dead man was lying on the ground. It was a horrible sight. He was hacked to pieces. I could not look".

About a year and a half later he dreamed the following:

"I saw two German soldiers with machine guns. One held the gun and the other fed the bullets. (It was in occupied land). I sneaked up and pushed them over the cliff".

The road which the patient had to traverse in that year and a half was indeed a difficult one, as a comparison of the two dreams indicates. The first dream reflects the basic anxiety which formed his attitude to reality situations and eventually brought him to analysis: fear of aggression, both from the outside world and from within himself. The second dream reveals the trend of change in his personality. He had reached the point where he felt that he could be aggressive and sadistic when necessary, handle guns, and even kill the enemy. Instead of running away from aggression, he was the aggressor. His conscious attitude and behavior at that time reflected the change expressed in the dream.

Analysts consider the first dream a patient produces in analysis to be of special importance, because it usually gives an indication of the patient's basic problem. (There are exceptions to this rule, however.)

The following is an illustration of a basic, "first" dream: (The patient is a young woman).

"I am walking with my little boy. Then I change into a little girl. My older sister holds me by the hand".

In the weeks following the dream, it became apparent that the patient's basic problem was the wish to remain a cute, seductive little girl and be taken care of as she wanted to be cared for in her childhood. From the time the patient was three, the older sister had been her substitute mother, a severe and punishing one. Walking with her little boy referred to her children, also to her bisexuality and wish to be a boy. Such a dream gives a clear indication of the long struggle ahead before the patient will mature emotionally and be able to be an adult in every respect, instead of being ill, which is the deepest expression of helplessness and the desire to be taken care of.

In the light of all that has been said about dreams and their importance, one may be inclined to press the patient for dreams and make him feel, as many do before coming for treatment, that analysis consists solely of dream interpretations. Analysts must guard against giving that impression, or overemphasizing to the patient the role of dreams. Cases have been brought to my attention of analysts telling patients that treatment was not progressing because they brought no dreams.

Before concluding, it is necessary to give a word of warning in regard to those dreams, the context of which may be frightening to the patient. Reference is made to dreams relating to deep, fundamental conflicts, for instance, homosexual tendencies, incest wishes, or death wishes concerning parents, spouse, or children. Such dreams are dangerous, charged as they are with explosive content which the patient may not be ready to accept and he may therefore be severely frightened. Postpone the analysis and interpretation of such dreams; dealing with them too early in the treatment interferes with the establishment of the transference relationship and may even frighten the patient away from analysis altogether.

Chapter X

PROBLEMS OF
COUNTER-TRANSFERENCE

In the foregoing pages frequent reference has been made to the analyst's attitude towards his patients. The ideal is that he be sympathetic and capable of identifying himself with the patient. Often, however, we are not quite up to that ideal. Feelings of annoyance and irritation may be aroused in the analyst by the patient's criticism and aggression, or on the other hand, too much sympathy, liking, and tenderness by positive transference and compliant behavior. Sometimes the patient's attitude creates anxiety in the analyst. All such feelings can disturb the treatment unless the analyst is able to refrain from displaying them. Lack of such control is always due to unresolved problems within the unconscious of the analyst.

Not much has been written about the analyst's counter-transference to his patient. Quite early in the development of psychoanalytic technique Freud remarked that "analysts have to learn to tolerate a measure of truth". He also stressed the necessity of the analyst's being able to control his feelings toward his patient and warned that he should not take the patient's positive transference as a reality. Ferenczi emphasized as one of the most important functions of the analyst, the ability to handle the counter-transference. He reminded us that the analyst was like everyone else in having sympathies and antipathies, both of which are necessary to feel and understand the patient's emotional problems. The analyst must do double duty: on one hand, observe his patient, weigh and understand what he says, and from his productions and behavior draw conclusions about his unconscious; at the same time he must be aware of and control his own attitude toward the patient. The patient's manner of speaking, the sound of his voice, his behavior, all affect the therapist.

How basically important it is that the analyst be aware of all these factors becomes apparent as one gains in experience. The analyst's failures, especially, teach him to appreciate the importance of knowing his own mental processes and emotional reactions. If he wants to understand the patient's unconscious, to sympathize with and be tolerant of the patient's attitudes, emotional productions, and behavior, he must have a sound knowledge of his own unconscious. He must be constantly aware of his counter-transference, be his feelings friendly or antagonistic.

In a previous chapter, mention was made of an analyst who was becoming irritated and bored with his patient's repetitious dreams and lack of progress. The analyst's irritation was a result of his *eagerness to cure*. To his unconscious the patient's repetitiousness meant interference with the realization of his desire.

Another beginning analyst dismissed a patient fifteen minutes before the session was over without realizing it. In the control hour it became apparent that he was annoyed with the patient. As he expressed it, he was "fed up". He was still in analysis himself and carried over his problems from his own analysis to the relationship with this patient. He was reluctant to analyze all the material his patient produced because he did not want to become aware of, and hence disturbed by, the same type of feeling in himself. He had had to deal mostly with transference material relating to the patient's Œdipus period. Because he could not evaluate objectively the transference feelings and actions of his patient, he began to respond to them as to a personal attitude towards him and hence he reacted with too much tension.

Another analyst made an appointment for his control session for an hour that coincided with an appointment he had made with his patient, completely forgetting the previous engagement. The analysis of this lapse of memory is too involved to reproduce here. It is obvious, however, that he did not want to see the patient. It took a long period of hard work, which involved taking a great deal of abuse from the patient before this slip was worked out and analysis resumed.

The analyst's attitude to his patients may be affected by overwork, stimulation of unconscious conflicts through the analytic material and, as Glover pointed out, by emotional frustration. A variety of cases exposes one to constantly changing feelings which may eventually provoke conflicts. The analyst who was "fed up" with his patient used his analysis of patients as an emotional outlet for many of his own problems. The fact that he was still in analysis and had not sufficiently resolved his own problems, was largely responsible for that situation.   His choice of psychiatric and analytic work had been neurotically determined.   For years before he came to analysis he had the need to work with neurotic patients because in that way he could externalize his own problems and, in giving all his attention to his patients' problems, he could avoid being preoccupied with his own.   He continued to do so for a long time in his analysis.   It was demonstrated to him that he constantly projected himself into his patients' lives and re-lived his own conflicts through their problems.   During an analytic hour he would, for instance, describe how easily one of his patients brought out incestuous material relating to her brother and father and how clearly she saw her acute death wishes against her mother.   Then I demonstrated to him that these were actually his own problems in reverse and that he intuitively sensed the meaning of his patient's productions in these instances because they touched on his own conflicts.   He became increasingly unhappy, dissatisfied, and bored with his work in the clinic and, whereas previously it had been his main pleasure, during this period of analysis he did not feel like going to the clinic at all and at times nearly fell asleep when he had his private patients. Even when his analysis had progressed to the point where he could do more effective work again, remnants of the neurotic fixation to his profession reappeared at times and caused slips similar to his sending the patient away too early.   In his case the main problem was that his own conflicts prevented him from viewing objectively the material produced by the patient.   Such strong, unresolved conflicts in the analyst can be the cause of untold difficulties in his analytical work.

Another important source of counter-transference reactions in the analyst is his *narcissism* which, if wounded, may produce feelings of resentment towards the patient. Sometimes the patient behaves in a way which seems to counteract the analyst's therapeutic aims; occasionally the patient acts contrary to the analyst's advice (one of the drawbacks of active interference). For instance, a patient may start to be promiscuous or may contemplate marriage or divorce. Some analysts react rigidly to such situations and may even declare to the patient that the treatment cannot continue if he carries out his desires. If the analyst considers the patient's behavior to be directed personally against his "aim to cure", he obviously is laboring under strong feelings of counter-transference. At times the patient cannot be prevented from acting in a way he chooses. Therefore the analyst's object must be to constantly analyze, interpret, and have the patient understand why he wants to make a change in his life. Sometimes, with the aid of candid objectivity, the analyst will find that such a change during analysis is not unusual and may even further the patient's progress.

Recently I had occasion to correct a colleague in supervised clinical work who was thinking of terminating the analysis of a young girl. She seemed to have made a satisfactory adjustment. However, her attitude to him was sarcastic and abusive; she was hardly ever able to express any positive feelings. Her dreams and fantasies showed a need for dependence, which the analyst failed to perceive because of his irritation with her negative transference.

If the analyst has a resentful attitude, he may try to

force interpretations on the patient. He may try to prove to the patient from the patient's dreams that his interpretations are correct despite the patient's rejection. Some analysts use silence as a means of revenge and behave as if they had a chip on their shoulder. They may feel that they have this prerogative, which of course carries the early childhood resentment of the parents' prerogative. In such cases analysis develops into a combat between doctor and patient, each trying to prove that the other is at fault.

Counter-transference manifestations which arise from the analyst's unconscious conflicts often bring about situations which are full of emotional tension and lead the patient to plan a change of analysts. Occasionally even the analyst himself considers it. It sometimes happens that the analyst has an antipathy for a patient (just as at the start he usually has a feeling of sympathy) but is not very clear as to why he feels that way. Some analysts are even ready to admit that they favor a certain type of patient. These therapists may be interested in some particular phase of analysis; they may have a strong curiosity due to unconscious sources which were not sufficiently resolved in their own analysis, and if the patient does not produce the expected material, symptoms, and results, the analyst is disappointed. He may feel it as a narcissistic injury, a questioning of his ability, a doubting of his potency. In such situations, if the analyst has strong feelings about the matter, the wisest thing for him to do is advise a change of analyst.

Little annoyances with his patients which the analyst overlooks temporarily can accumulate and result in the development of strong feelings of hostility towards them. In turn these feelings may give rise to a rigid and frustrating attitude, which the patient may recognize. Such situations as the patient's over-staying and the analyst's being embarrassed to mention it, the patient's frequent request to change appointments, or use the telephone, and the like, all interfere with the analyst's convenience and if not analyzed may accumulate and strengthen his negative counter-transference. I have found that this is also true in regard to discussing fees. In supervised clinical work I have frequently had to draw the attention of the analyst to his "blind spot" regarding material presented by the patient which concerned financial problems and point out to the analyst that it was caused by his own insecurity in handling the matter of fees. It is always advisable to discuss payment of fees with the patient when arranging for treatment. Some young colleagues are uncertain as to what arrangements to make. Some request payment in advance, being afraid that the patient may terminate analysis and refuse to pay the bill. Obviously, that is a bad arrangement, the main reason for which is the analyst's insecurity and distrust of his own ability, but other unconscious reasons are also at work. Should one charge the patient when he stays away and claims that he was sick? It must be explained to the patient that he is hiring a certain amount of the analyst's time for which he must pay, even if he does not come. After that basic understanding is reached, the analyst can be elastic about charging for absence on account of illness. Experience is again the teacher in such matters; the analyst becomes more spontaneous in handling them as he goes along.

In the case of analysts who are just beginning practice, personal elements may enter strongly into their work and create anxiety which can seriously interfere with the effectiveness of therapy. For instance, when an impotent patient began to complain of the harmful effects of analysis at a period when his night-emissions became frequent, the analyst interrupted to reassure him that they were caused by the particular phase of analysis they had reached and that they would pass. What he should have done was to encourage the patient to continue speaking about the aggravated symptom so that its unconscious meaning could be determined. The analyst's reassurance, which was based on his inability to tolerate even temporary discomfort on the part of the patient, interfered with the progress of treatment. Another colleague had a patient who was in a depressed mood, complained about it, and then lapsed into silence. The therapist did not question the patient or otherwise encourage him to talk. He was really relieved by the silence. When asked in the control hour about his attitude he replied: "The patient knew that he was depressed because of his hostility so I saw no need to question him". Through further probing of his reluctance to discuss the patient's mood with him, it became evident that he himself was slightly depressed and was afraid to be reminded of the reasons for it. Obviously, analysis cannot proceed under such circumstances.

The analytic situation is created by the *patient's transference to the analyst and by the analyst's various attitudes to the patient.* These attitudes become ap-

parent through the manner in which the analyst gives
his interpretations, the length of time he uses for
them, etc. His communications may be short and
rigid or lengthy and elastic. His attitude may also be
expressed through silence. It is true that in spite of
the counter-transference phenomenon patients do
progress. They bring up reactions to the analyst's
attitude (if they are permitted) but difficulties for
both patient and analyst can be avoided if the analyst
is aware of his feelings towards the patients. The
analyst's personality always enters into the treatment
to an extent, but if he is too subjective and the
therapeutic process creates a strong emotional reaction within him, progress is seriously hindered. At
times physicians in control analysis, who have not
yet completed their own analysis, feel somewhat inhibited in regard to analyzing the sexual transference
of their patients. Under those circumstances the analysis becomes tiresome work. Such was also the case
with the young colleague mentioned above, who dismissed his patient by mistake fifteen minutes early.

Counter-transference reactions are more likely to
disturb the progress of analysis in cases where analysts
have not had sufficient experience. It does no follow,
however, that experienced analysts do not occasionally
meet with such difficulties with certain patients. A
colleague was at times extremely disturbed when his
patients were not in a talkative mood. On such occasions he was conscious of wishing that the patient
would leave. "They make me feel frustrated, hope-
less", he said. This reaction resulted from his unconscious, repressed feelings related to infantile experiences. He felt frustrated in his attempts to progress

with treatment if the patient was silent and he believed
that he was not liked by the patient; just as in childhood he had many times experienced situations in
which not being talked to meant being in disfavor.

One can see from the above examples how the
analyst can unconsciously associate personal aims with
therapeutic aims. Analysis served to gratify this physician's narcissism. His case also illustrates the importance of eliminating, during training, the analyst's
personality difficulties. It is not sufficient for him to
get a glimpse of his unconscious and his emotional
problems. If that is all that is accomplished the analyst's problems are worked out in his relationships
with his patients, with ill effect, of course. He cannot
achieve the needed identification with his patients nor
can he evaluate objectively their behavior and productions. For that reason he may fail to understand
the emotions which keep a patient silent, for instance.
Or, towards the close of analysis he may become annoyed with a patient for re-exhibiting neurotic symptoms which were previously cleared up, even though
the analyst knows theoretically that the recurrence
may well be a defense reaction to the completion of
treatment and separation from the analyst. That
aspect is overlooked and the behavior is taken as aggression towards him personally.

On the other hand, some therapists become too
involved in the patient's emotional reactions in a positive way. One analyst complained to me about his
being too mild, liking his patients and pitying them,
to the extent that at times he was moved to tears by
one patient's constant crying (a case of hysterical depression which was under discussion at that time).

This over-emotional attitude to the patient made it difficult for him to appreciate the negative, aggressive feelings which the patient had as a result of being frustrated in analysis. He could not see indications of them in the patient's productions, failed to recognize them even in the dreams. He did analyze aggression and resentment, but always in relationship to reality and early childhood objects, neglecting the transference relationship. It turned out that he was really afraid of the patient's strong aggression. He feared all aggression, considering it a personal attack. Another variation of this attitude is the analyst's constant prodding of the patient to elicit aggression in the transference. In such cases it is frequently found that the analyst has too much unresolved masochism.

Many analysts emphasize educational aspects by their attitudes and interpretations, and imply through instructions and warnings that the patient can come up to their level if he follows their advice. I knew an analyst who had a habit of walking around the reservoir in the park every morning and used to prescribe it for some of his patients. Indirectly he was saying: "See how much I have achieved through discipline. Imitate me and you, too, will be a success". This belongs in the same category with the analyst who tries to convince his patients that their complaints and reactions are exaggerated and dramatic. Patients sometimes challenge the analyst to give such an opinion by asking: "Don't I act hysterical? Doesn't it sound dramatic?" It is of course important for the analyst to know how much educational work should enter into the analysis. It is even more difficult for him to know how much severity or mildness he should express in the course of treatment. Again, he learns those by experience. Utmost caution must be practised until one achieves the proper balance.

The greatest danger in not paying enough attention to counter-transference manifestations is that analysis can become a boring process for the analyst. Sooner or later the patient senses it; moreover, consciously or unconsciously, the analyst's conduct will be such that termination of analysis is unavoidable. It is much better to admit to the patient that at times he is tiresome or even boring than to harbor unconscious resentment and feelings of wanting to get rid of him.

I mentioned earlier in this volume that analysis is an emotional experience for the patient; it is an emotional experience for the analyst as well. It can be a disturbing one where the analyst is lacking in elasticity and is not able to tolerate the patient's criticism. In beginning analysts I have found the tendency to use their own analysis as a completely unalterable sample with all their cases. That practice hinders the development of elasticity. It is therefore of great importance that clinical seminars and supervised clinical work be conducted by different analysts. Through contact with many experienced physicians during the training period, the young analyst learns different modes of approach and various ways of handling certain situations and material; and his ability and effectiveness are increased thereby.

The counter-transference implications of the acceptance of gifts from patients form another important problem that has to be seriously considered by the beginning practitioner of analysis. I have had to rectify quite a few situations where treatment did not and could not progress because of the analyst's accepting a gift from the patient or, on rare occasions, giving one to the patient. The analysts who became thus involved usually stated, and with some justification, that they did not have the opportunity of learning to handle such matters because it was not a problem in their own analysis and they did not hear it discussed at seminars.

I am not referring to instances where the patient impulsively sends flowers or a book or some other trifle, without having previously discussed it in analysis. In such cases the only thing to do is to receive it graciously. However, the patient's action must be analyzed as thoroughly as possible and he should be brought to realize that, although it is a gesture of affection or an attempt at bribery, at the same time (as the patient knows from his own experience), he also harbors feelings of hostility and aggression towards the analyst. And although he was not aware of them just at the moment of sending the gift, they are nevertheless there because analysis is still in progress. The sending of a trifling gift may be an impulsive action and the feelings which prompted it can very easily change later, involving no embarrassment for the analyst.

It occasionally happens, however, that an analyst receives a valuable gift from a patient while analysis is still in progress. At the time of presentation the gift may appear to be an expression of pure gratitude, but clearly its object is to insure a continuation of the analyst's benevolent attitude. It always is related to the patient's infantile drives and his desire to bribe the analyst. There are numerous other unconscious reasons as well. Such has always been the case in the situations brought to my attention in supervised clinical work. The acceptance of an expensive present will inhibit the patient's progress because the analyst who accepts it is very rarely willing to fully analyze every aspect of the situation. Even if he works through all the above-mentioned reasons he will still owe an explanation for his own acceptance of it.

One colleague who was being supervised by me, justified the acceptance of a gift by saying that the patient did not pay him enough anyway and he therefore felt entitled to it. (He had, however, never discussed with the patient the fact that he felt he was being underpaid). In another instance, the same type of explanation was given with the added comment that "the patient is nasty and abusive and has enough money besides". In this case also the analyst failed to discuss with the patient the matter of raising his fee.

In other cases more embarrassment followed as time went on because the analyst felt that his hands were tied by the patient's generous gesture. It inhibited his interpretations and a period of stagnation followed. In all these instances the situation was corrected when the analyst finally decided to deduct the price of the gift from the patient's bill, assuring the patient of appreciation, while explaining to him that such a gift can only be accepted long after analysis is finished, if the patient still feels so inclined.

No matter how satisfactorily the analyst can rationalize to himself his acceptance of an expensive gift, it is still due to deep, unconscious problems concerning giving and taking which were not clarified and successfully worked out in his own analysis.

Chapter XI

TERMINATION

As in the case of counter-transference manifestations, the literature on the problem of when and how to terminate an analysis is meager. How long an analysis should last and what success one will achieve depends on many factors: the type of neurosis, the intensity of the emotional drives involved, and the strength and variety of defenses which must be eliminated in the course of treatment.

It seems logical to view the problem from the standpoint of the ætiology of the neurosis. For each type of neurosis there are different criteria for determining: progress of therapy, degree of adjustment, and indications for termination. The improvement which it is possible to make in hysterias and anxiety neuroses differs from that which can be effected in a compulsive neurotic. Similarly the extent to which a person with sexual difficulties can be helped differs markedly from the results in character neuroses. Finally, neurotic depressions must be considered in a class by themselves.

The patient becomes ill because reality is experienced as a hardship and a continuation of childhood frustrations. His parents have treated him harshly, without understanding. In analysis he learns to understand, through the transference, his past and present emotional entanglements and relationships. Through the analyst's benevolent attitude he realizes that it is possible to be treated differently than he was in the past and he also loses his fear of the world. All this comes at a slow pace and dynamic emotional changes together with structural ones are made. A new distribution of energies takes place and the patient becomes more relaxed and satisfied than he was before analysis.

One can best judge by one's own experiences with patients whom one has had the opportunity to observe after their analysis has been terminated, whether the changes which took place in the patient's behavior were reliable criteria for finishing analysis.

In a questionnaire edited by Edward Glover [1] the majority of analysts participating stated that their criteria for termination were mainly intuitive. I believe the term was meant to include their understanding that the patient's behavior indicated his ability to adjust well if dismissed from treatment. It is a good practice to follow up as many patients as possible. In that way it can be determined whether analysis was terminated at the proper time.

Setting a date seems to be the most usual way of ending treatment, although Freud warned that if the date was afterwards changed, the aim of analysis might be injured thereby. "If one hits the right time at which to employ it", he said, "it can be effective. Only, never change, and if the patient has to continue, let him continue with another analyst".

If one sets a date with a view to putting pressure on the patient to bring in more material, that effect may be achieved, but when the term expires the analyst

[1] *An Investigation of the Technique of Psychoanalysis*, edited by Edward Glover, M.D. The William and Wilkins Co., Baltimore, 1940.

may find that the patient still has important problems to work out and cannot be sent away. If, however, one is not arbitrary and sets a date in the form of a casual suggestion, in the same manner in which other active measures of technique are used (of which many examples were cited in preceding chapters), the analyst will be in a position to continue analysis if he deems it advisable. At an opportune moment one may casually say, for instance, "I don't think we shall continue treatment after your summer vacation", or, "I think you may be finished with your analysis by summer". Then if the patient needs further help, we can simply state that it seems necessary to go on with treatment. So far this method has always worked satisfactorily with my patients.

Often patients themselves bring up the matter of terminating treatment by asking how much longer they will need to come. Sometimes they are more definite and may state, for instance, that they will not come back in the fall. That gives the analyst an opportunity to discuss a tentative time limit for winding up the analysis.

It is very possible that no two analysts have exactly the same methods and criteria for finishing treatment. Setting a time limit may be appropriate in some cases but in others it may have the effect of prolonging analysis. The most desirable state of affairs is for the patient to slowly wean himself away, for him to eventually accept his limitations and be willing to relinquish the desires which cannot be realized.

The degree of improvement which the treatment has brought about is judged differently by individual analysts. In my opinion, the following should be given primary consideration in determining the patient's ability to leave analysis:

First, ability to work and find greater satisfaction in it than before analysis.

Second, less fear of social contacts and a generally more outgoing attitude.

Third, ability to find more enjoyment in life, which of course includes a healthier and more pleasurable sexual adjustment.

In the case of patients whose chief objective in coming to analysis is a solution of sexual difficulties, that sphere is the first to be considered as the test of success of treatment and as the sign that analysis can be brought to a close.

Nineteen years ago I analyzed a young man who was impotent. His occupation of furrier carried fetishistic gratifications which slowed the progress of analysis. However, in the advanced stage of analysis he was able to give up his masturbatory activities and strong exhibitionistic tendencies and began to adjust to a more adult sexual life. Therefore after his third year I terminated his analysis. I later found out that he had made an excellent adjustment: shortly after analysis he went into business for himself, married, and raised a family.

Another patient whom I treated seventeen years ago (whose abbreviated case history was presented in the chapter on anxiety hysteria) finished his treatment by gradually weaning himself. After about two and one-half years of intensive analysis he reduced the frequency of his visits to three times a week. He terminated the analysis himself by not returning after his summer vacation, a plan he had discussed often in the spring months. I have been in contact with him since. He has never had a relapse and is very well adjusted in every respect.

A patient suffering from anxiety who was in treatment about nine years ago had seventeen months of analysis, after which he was well advanced in many respects, better able to handle all his problems, especially his anxieties. I did not consider his analysis completed and he himself planned to come back the following year, but was unable to arrange to be in New York. After terminating he continued to improve; he is well adjusted, works steadily, has satisfactory sexual and social relationships and has never felt the need for further analysis. His case is a good example of the type of patient with whom deep penetration to the earliest infantile sources is not absolutely necessary.

In the case of a woman who was in treatment with me seven years ago, the analysis was terminated after eighteen months because family matters required her presence in another part of the country. The termination was fixed for the beginning of the summer when she was to leave town. When we met, years later, she stated that one more year of analysis would have saved her the five years it took her to work out her problems in accordance with the insight she had gained from the year and a half of analytic treatment.

Many of the symptoms of the latter two patients disappeared completely during analysis but they still had difficulties which were ironed out after their analysis was terminated.

At times one has to be satisfied with partial success

and must accept the fact that no more can be done for the patient. In some cases failure to terminate analysis soon enough may over-intensify the attachment to the analyst, and lead the patient to expect the impossible. The practical results: the reduction of symptoms and extreme peculiar actions and reactions should guide the analyst in his decision to terminate treatment. During treatment the analyst observes the patient, collecting data on his activities and behavior, and can judge how much more tolerant of frustration the patient becomes. In addition, the constantly changing reactions in the transference and the continual reports about the patient's social life and work should enable the analyst to judge where the patient stands at any time. Furthermore, the dream material reflects changes in the unconscious.

In the course of treatment there are always indications of the patient's progress or lack of it. The strength and variety of defenses are a reliable guide to the strength of the tendencies to escape from the newly tried relationships. One can watch in the course of treatment the gradual reduction of tendencies to regress and escape reality and observe how the patient learns through his experience in the transference relationship to be more courageous, and to react with less anxiety to situations which he previously tried to entirely avoid.

An important criterion for termination is the changing character of the patient's object relationships. Very often the most one is able to accomplish is a change in the patient's attitude rather than a change in character. During analysis the patient reacts strongly to frustrations and displays extreme intolerance of family members whom he looks upon as the cause of all his sufferings. When he becomes tolerant of these "guilty" individuals, it is one of the most important signs of progress. In the five-year analysis of the patient with anorexia nervosa (cited in the chapter on neurotic depression) a friendly relationship with the family members and the external world had to be established. This was a difficult task because bringing her to that point marked *the first time in her life* that she was able to feel friendly towards anyone. Prior to analysis all her relationships had been hostile. That attitude was expressed in her neurosis, her symptoms, and in the tendency to withdraw from the family and the world.

One can forecast the results of analysis on the basis of the quality of object relationship and the degree of elasticity and tolerance before analysis. The better the object relationships and the greater the flexibility, the shorter the analysis.

As mentioned previously, the patient's dreams give reliable indications of progress and approach to the time for termination. A young woman whose outstanding problem was sexual frigidity had the following dream a few weeks prior to the termination of analysis:

> "I was in a room. I knew I would be gassed together with other people. I thought I was going to die. I did not know whether I should save myself."

and a second dream the same night:

"I was walking with another girl in a Colored section. Suddenly the girl was snatched away and disappeared."

Both dreams concerned her sexual problem: they express the desire for sexual relationships. In the first dream being gassed meant sexual orgasm and losing consciousness. Thinking of death expresses the same idea. The doubt as to whether to save herself represented her acceptance of the feminine attitude concerning sex, to an extent never before expressed in her dreams. Actually, at the time of these dreams (the end of three years of treatment) her social.contacts and working ability, which had been at low ebb when she came to analysis, were entirely satisfactory. She had many admirers and several offers of marriage.

In the second dream, the Negro section refers to sexual freedom and passion by which she desires to be carried away. In neither dream does the old fear of sex and men appear. However, in the manifest dream content being gassed and kidnapped is an expression of a feeble attempt on the part of her unconscious to counteract the steadily growing, conscious sexual desire.

Ferenczi's standard for a successful analysis was that: "In every male patient the signs that his castration anxiety has been mastered must be forthcoming. And this sign is a sense of equality of rights with the analyst; and every female patient, if the cure is to be ranked as complete and permanent, must have finally conquered her masculinity complex and become able to submit without bitterness to thinking in terms of her feminine role."[1] That goal cannot always be achieved since all cases are not equally amenable to therapy. When we speak of cures in analysis we usually think in terms of having exposed the earliest roots of the neurosis and having brought the patient to recognize and face all the repressed material which is then worked through, demonstrating to him the influence of the unconscious impulses on his current behavior. Thus are eliminated the conflicts which have created and maintained disharmony between ego, superego, and id. Moreover, these three parts of the personality undergo alterations during the process of working through the repressed drives. The ego should become stronger, less fearful, less guilty, the superego more tolerant, less demanding, and less threatening, so that more id drives are permitted gratification. However, the severity of the neurotic illness, unfavorable constitutional factors, advanced age, all may counteract the effort of analysis to make the patient more flexible and elastic. When these factors are pronounced the patient's ego cannot be transformed in the desired manner.

Some analysts over-estimate therapeutic possibilities, just as all patients usually have exaggerated ideas of what analysis will do for them. The analyst must remember that psychoanalytic treatment is not a panacea for all ills. He should be able to decide whether the maximum has been accomplished in his cure and whether the patient has gained enough to manage by himself. When he has done as much as

[1] "Das Problem der Beendigung der Analysen", *Int. Ztschr. Psa.*, Band XIV, 1928.

it is possible to do, he should be aware of that fact and he must also bring the patient to the realization that there is no point in continuing, that it would be better for him to leave and try to utilize the knowledge he has already acquired. Therapeutic success must be measured in relation to "normal behavior". It should be borne in mind that in so-called normal behavior, everyone has special characteristics and peculiarities, even "neurotic" symptoms. When examined in that light, therapeutic results can be seen to be quite successful even if the patient retains some of his earlier patterns.

In such cases especially, when terminating treatment, the analyst must give the patient the feeling that his (the analyst's) door is always open. My experience has been that patients rarely come back for more analysis. Apparently, even with the above-mentioned handicaps, they progress enough to be able to cope with the difficulties for which they previously had to seek help.

Termination should always be based on our practical evidence of the patient's improvement. As Glover so justly says: "We are first and last clinical psychologists; we should be well advised to base our estimates of success first of all on clinical evidence and not on any theoretical preconceptions". [1]

[1] *An Investigation of the Technique of Psychoanalysis,* ed. by Edward Glover, M.D. The Williams and Wilkins Co., Baltimore, 1940.

BIBLIOGRAPHY

Key for Abbreviations

Int. Ztschr. Psa. ..*Internationale Zeitschrift fuer Psychoanalyse*
Int. J. Psa. ....*International Journal of Psychoanalysis*
Int. Psa. Verlag.... Internationaler Psychoanalytischer Verlag
J. Abnormal Psych. ......*Journal of Abnormal Psychology*
Psych. Quart. ....*The Psychoanalytic Quarterly*
Psych. Review.................*The Psychoanalytic Review*

ABRAHAM, KARL. *Selected Papers.* Trans. by Clement A.
Douglas Bryan and Alice Strachey. London: Institute
of Psychoanalysis and Hogarth Press. Int. Psa. Library
Series, No. 13, 1927.
———— A Peculiar Form of Neurotic Resistance Against
the Psychoanalytic Method. *Ibid.*
ALEXANDER, FRANZ. A Metapsychological Description of the
Process of Cure. *Int. J. Psa.*, vol. VI, pp. 13–34, *Abs.* by
John Rickman. 1923.
———— *Psychoanalysis of the Total Personality.* London,
Hogarth Press, 1927.
———— The Neurotic Character. *Int. J. Psa.*, vol. XI, 1930.
———— The Problem of Psychoanalytic Technique. *Psych.
Quart.*, vol. IV, 1935.
———— Psychoanalysis Comes of Age. *Psych. Quart.*, vol.
VII, 1938.
———— Psychoanalysis Revised. *Psych. Quart.*, vol. IX,
1940.
BALINT, ALICE, AND MICHAEL. On Transference and Counter-
Transference. *Int. J. Psa.*, vol. XX, 1939.
BALINT, MICHAEL. The Final Goal of Psychoanalytic Treat-
ment. *Int. J. Psa.*, vol. XVII, 1936.
———— Ego Strength and Education of the Ego. *Psych.
Quart.*, vol. XI, 1942.

BENEDEK, THERESE. Defense Mechanisms and Structure of the Total Personality. *Psych. Quart.*, vol. VI, 1937.

BERGLER, EDMUND. On the Resistance Situation: The Patient is Silent. *Psych. Review*, vol. 25, 1938.

———— Symposium on the Theory of Therapeutic Results of Psychoanalysis. *Ibid.*

BIBRING, EDUARD. Symposium on the Theory of Therapeutic Results of Psychoanalysis. *Ibid.*

BIBRING–LEHNER, GRETE. A Contribution to the Subject of Transference Resistance. *Int. J. Psa.*, vol. XVII, 1936, pp. 181–189.

BLANCO, IGNAZIO MATTE. Some Reflections on Psycho-Dynamics. *Int. J. Psa.*, vol. XXI, 1940.

BOEHM, FELIX. Duerfen wir Gefaelligkeiten von Patienten annehmen? *Int. Ztschr. Psa.*, vol. IX, 1923, p. 77.

———— Das Unbewusste des Analytikers in der Analyse. *Ibid.*

BREUER, JOSEF, AND FREUD, SIGMUND. *Studien ueber Hysterie.* Leipzig and Vienna. Franz Deuticke, 1895.

BRIERLEY, MARJORIE. Affects in Theory and Practice. *Int. J. Psa.*, vol. XVIII, 1937.

BRILL, A. A. A Few Remarks on the Technique of Psychoanalysis. *Medical Review of Reviews*, April, 1912.

————Facts and Fancies in Psychoanalytic Treatment. *Arch. of Neurol. and Psychiatry*, vol. II, No. 2, 1913, p. 230.

———— *Psychoanalysis. Its Theories and Practical Application.* Philadelphia and London: W. B. Saunders Co., 1913.

BRUNSWICK, RUTH MACK. A Supplement to Freud's History of an Infantile Neurosis. *Int. J. Psa.*, vol. IX, 1928.

BULLARD, DEXTER M. Experiences in the Psychoanalytic Treatment of Psychotics. *Psych. Quart.*, vol. IX, 1940.

CLARK, L. PIERCE. Some Practical Remarks upon the Use of Modified Psychoanalysis in the Treatment of Borderland Neuroses and Psychoses. *Psych. Review*, vol. VI, 1919, pp. 306–308.

COHN, FRANZ S. Practical Approach to the Problem of Narcissistic Neuroses. *Psych. Quart.*, vol. IX, 1940.

CORIAT, ISADOR H. Active Therapy in Psychoanalysis. *Psych. Review*, vol. XI, 1924, pp. 28–38.

—————— A Type of Anal-Erotic Resistance. *Int. J. Psa.*, vol. VII, 1926, pp. 392–395.

DEFOREST, IZETTE. The Therapeutic Technique of Sandor Ferenczi. *Int. J. Psa.*, vol. XXIII, 1942.

DEUTSCH, HELENE. *Psychoanalysis of the Neuroses.* London: Hogarth Press, 1933.

—————— A Discussion of Certain Forms of Resistance. *Int. J. Psa.*, vol. XX, 1939.

—————— *Psychology of Woman.* New York: Grune and Stratton, 1944, 2 vols.

EDER, M. D. Dreams as Resistance. *Int. J. Psa.*, vol. XI, 1930.

EIDELBERG, LUDWIG. Pseudo-Identification. *Int. J. Psa.*, vol. XIX, 1938.

EITINGON, MAX. Ueber neuere Methoden-Kritik an der Psychoanalyse. *Int. Ztschr. Psa.*, vol. XVII, 1931, pp. 5–15.

EMCH, MINNA. On 'The Need to Know' as Related to Identification and Acting Out. *Int. J. Psa.*, vol. XXV, 1944.

FEDERN, PAUL. An Every-Day Compulsion. *Int. J. Psa.*, vol. X, 1929.

FENICHEL, OTTO. *Outline of Clinical Psychoanalysis.* New York: W. W. Norton and Co., 1932.

—————— Zur Theorie der psychoanalytischen Technik. *Int. Ztschr. Psa.*, vol. XXI, 1935, pp. 78–95.

—————— Symposium on the Theory of the Therapeutic Results of Psychoanalysis. *Int. J. Psa.*, vol. XVIII, 1937.

—————— Ego-Disturbances and their Treatment. *Int. J. Psa.*, vol. XIX, 1938.

—————— Problems of Psychoanalytic Technique. Parts I–V. *Psych. Quart.*, vols. VII and VIII, 1938, 1939.

FERENCZI, SANDOR. *Contributions to Psychoanalysis.* Auth. Trans. by Ernest Jones. Boston: Richard G. Badger. 1916, pp. 288.

———— *The Development of Psychoanalysis*. Auth. Trans. by Caroline Newton. Nervous and Mental Disease Pub. Co. Monograph Series, No. 40, 1925, pp. 68.

———— *Further Contributions to the Theory and Technique of Psychoanalysis*. London: Institute of Psychoanalysis and Hogarth Press. Compiled by John Rickman. Auth. Trans. by Jane Isabel Suttie, and others. 1926, pp. 473.

———— The Unwelcome Child and His Death Instinct. *Int. J. Psa.*, vol. X, 1929.

———— The Principle of Relaxation and Neocatharsis. *Int. J. Psa.*, vol. XI, 1930.

———— Child Analysis in the Analysis of Adults. *Int. J. Psa.*, vol. XII, 1931.

FERENCZI, SANDOR AND RANK, OTTO. Die Elastizitaet der psychoanalytischen Technik. *Int. Ztschr. Psa.*, vol. XIV, 1928, pp. 197–209.

FLIESS, ROBERT. The Metapsychology of the Analyst. *Psych. Quart.*, vol. XI, 1942.

FORSYTH, DAVID. *The Technique of Psychoanalysis*. London: Kegan, Paul, Ltd. New York: Moffat, Yard and Co., 1922, pp. 133.

FRENCH, THOMAS M. A Clinical Study of Learning in the Course of a Psychoanalytic Treatment. *Psych. Quart.*, vol. V, 1936.

———— Reality Testing in Dreams. *Psych. Quart.*, vol. VI, 1937.

———— Insight and Distortion in Dreams. *Int. J. Psa.*, vol. XX, 1939.

———— Ego Analysis as a Guide to Therapy. *Psych. Quart.*, vol. XIV, 1945.

FREUD, ANNA. *The Technique of Child Analysis*. New York and Washington: Nerv. and Ment. Dis. Pub. Co., 1928.

———— *The Ego and the Mechanisms of Defense*. London: Hogarth Press, 1937.

FREUD, SIGMUND. The Psychotherapy of Hysteria. Auth. Trans. by A. A. Brill. Freud: *Selected Papers on Hysteria*.

Nervous and Mental Disease Monograph Series, No. 4, 1895.

———— Observations on "Wild" Psychoanalysis. Auth. Trans. by A. A. Brill, 1909. *Collected Papers,* vol. II. Hogarth Press, London, 1924.

———— On Psychotherapy. Auth. Trans. by A. A. Brill, 1909. *Collected Papers,* vol. I, 1924.

———— The Future Chances of Psychoanalytic Therapy. Auth. Trans. by A. A. Brill, 1909. *Collected Papers,* vol. II, 1924.

———— On Psychoanalysis. *Amer. J. Psych.* 1910.

———— *Three Contributions to Theory of Sex.* New York: Nerv. and Ment. Dis. Pub. Co., 1910.

———— *The Interpretation of Dreams.* London: Allen and Unwin, 1915.

———— A Child Is Being Beaten. A Contribution to the Study of the Origin of Sexual Perversions. Trans. by Alix Strachey and James Strachey. *Collected Papers,* vol. II, 1924.

———— One of the Difficulties of Psychoanalysis. *Int. J. Psa.,* vol. I, pp. 17-23. Trans. by Joan Riviere. *Collected Papers,* vol. IV, 1924.

———— *Group Psychology and the Analysis of the Ego.* Auth. Trans. by James Strachey, Int. Psa. Press, London, 1922.

————Character and Anal Erotism. Trans. by R. C. McWatters. *Collected Papers,* vol. II, 1924.

———— Further Recommendations in the Technique of Psychoanalysis. Trans. by Joan Riviere. *Ibid.*

———— Neurosis and Psychosis. Trans. by Joan Riviere. *Ibid.*

————Obsessions and Phobias: Their Psychical Mechanism and Their Aetiology. Trans. by M. Meyer. *Collected Papers,* vol. I, 1924.

———— Obsessive Acts and Religious Practices. Trans. by R. C. McWatters. *Collected Papers,* vol. II, 1924.

———— Recommendations for Physicians on the Psychoanalytic Method of Treatment. Trans. by Joan Riviere. *Ibid.*

———— Repression. Trans. by Cecil M. Baines. *Collected Papers,* vol. IV, 1924.

———— The Dynamics of the Transference. Trans. by Joan Riviere. *Collected Papers,* vol. II, 1924.

———— The Infantile Genital Organization of the Libido. *Int. J. Psa.,* vol. V, pp. 125–129. Trans. by Joan Riviere. *Collected Papers,* vol. II, 1924.

———— The Passing of the Oedipus Complex. *Int. J. Psa.,* vol. V, pp. 419–423. Trans. by Joan Riviere. *Collected Papers,* vol. II, 1924.

———— The Predisposition to Obsessional Neurosis. Trans. by Edward George Glover and E. Colburn Mayne. *Collected Papers,* vol. II, 1924.

———— Turnings in the Ways of Psychoanalytic Therapy. Trans. by Joan Riviere. *Collected Papers,* vol. II, 1924.

———— Fragment of an Analysis of a Case of Hysteria. Trans. by Alix Strachey and James Strachey. *Collected Papers,* vol. III, 1925.

———— Metapsychological Supplement to the Theory of Dreams. Trans. by Cecil M. Baines. *Collected Papers,* vol. IV, 1925.

———— Mourning and Melancholia. Trans. by Joan Riviere. *Ibid.*

———— Notes Upon a Case of Obsessional Neurosis. Trans. by Alix Strachey and James Strachey. *Collected Papers,* vol. III, 1925.

———— *New Introductory Lectures on Psychoanalysis.* London, Hogarth Press, 1933.

———— *The Ego and the Id.* Auth. Trans. by Joan Riviere. London: Institute of Psychoanalysis and Hogarth Press, 1927.

———— *A General Introduction to Psychoanalysis.* New York. Liveright Publishing Corp., 1935.

———— *The Problem of Anxiety.* New York. W. W. Norton and Co., 1936.

————Analysis Terminable and Interminable. *Int. J. Psa.,* vol. XVIII, 1937.

———— Constructions in Analysis. *Int. J. Psa.,* vol. XIX, 1938.

———— Splitting of the Ego in the Defensive Process. *Int. J. Psa.,* vol. XXII, 1941.

———— Remarks Upon the Theory and Practice of Dream Interpretation. *Int. J. Psa.,* vol. XXIV, 1943.

———— Some Additional Notes Upon Dream Interpretation As a Whole. *Int. J. Psa.,* vol. XXIV, 1943.

————Fausse Reconnaissance (Déjà Raconté) in Psychoanalytic Treatment. *Collected Papers,* vol. II, 1924.

———— The Employment of Dream Interpretation in Psychoanalysis. *Ibid.*

————Analysis of a Phobia in a Five-Year-Old Boy. *Collected Papers,* vol. III, 1924.

———— From the History of an Infantile Neurosis. *Ibid.*

———— On Narcissism: An Introduction. *Collected Papers,* vol. IV, 1924.

————Some Character Types Met with in Psychoanalytic Work. *Ibid.*

FRINK, H. W. *Morbid Fears and Compulsions. Their Psychology and Psychoanalytic Treatment.* With an Introduction by J. J. Putnam. New York: Moffat, Yard and Co. London: Kegan, Paul and Co., 1918.

FROMM-REICHMAN, FRIEDA. Transference Problems in Schizophrenics. *Psych. Quart.,* vol. VIII, 1939.

GERO, GEORGE. The Construction of Depression. *Int. J. Psa.,* vol. XVII, 1936.

GLOVER, EDWARD. 'Active Therapy' and Psychoanalysis. *Int. J. Psa.,* vol. V, 1924, pp. 269–311.

———— A 'Technical' Form of Resistance. *Int. J. Psa.,* vol. VII, 1926, pp. 377–389.

———— Lectures on Technique in Psychoanalysis. *Int. J. Psa.,* vol. VIII, 1927.

————— Lectures on Technique in Psychoanalysis (continued). *Int. J. Psa.*, vol. IX, 1928.

————— The 'Vehicle' of Interpretations. *Int. J. Psa.*, vol. XI, 1930.

————— A Development Study of the Obsessional Neurosis. *Int. J. Psa.*, vol. XVI, 1935.

————— Symposium on the Theory of the Therapeutic Results of Psychoanalysis. *Int. J. Psa.*, vol. XVIII, 1937.

GREENACRE, PHYLLIS. The Predisposition to Anxiety. *Psych. Quart.*, vol. X, 1941.

————— The Predisposition to Anxiety, Part II. *Ibid.*

HANN-KENDE, FANNY. Zur Uebertragung und Gegenuebertragung in der Psychoanalyse. *Int. Ztschr. Psa.*, vol. XII, 1926, pp. 478–486.

HARNIK, J. WITH K. ABRAHAM. Special Pathology and Therapy of the Neuroses and Psychoses. *Int. J. Psa.*, vol. I, 1920, pp. 280–285.

HARNIK, J. Ueber die Forcierung blasphemischer Fantasien. *Int. Ztschr. Psa.*, vol. XIII, 1927, pp. 61–64.

————— Resistance to the Interpretation of Dreams in Analysis. *Int. J. Psa.*, vol. XI, 1930, pp. 75–78.

HARTMANN, HEINZ. *Die Grundlagen der Psychoanalyse.* Leipzig: Georg Thieme, 1927.

————— Psychoanalysis and the Concept of Health. *Int. J. Psa.*, vol. XX, 1939.

HENDRICK, IVES. *Facts and Theories of Psychoanalysis.* New York. Alfred A. Knopf, 1934.

HERMANN, IMRE. *Die Psychoanalyse als Methode.* Vienna: Int. Psa. Verlag. 1934.

HEROLD, CARL M. A Controversy About Technique. *Psych. Quart.*, vol. VIII, 1939.

HILL, LEWIS B. The Use of Hostility as Defense. *Psych. Quart.*, vol. VII, 1938.

HITSCHMANN, EDUARD. Die Indikationen fuer psychoanalytische Behandlung. Vienna, *Ars Medici*, vol. XIV, No. 10, 1924.

HORNEY, K. Die Technik der psychoanalytischen Therapie. *Zeitschrift f. Sexualwissenschaft*, vol. IV, 1917, p. 185.

———— The Problem of the Negative Therapeutic Reaction. *Psych. Quart.*, vol. V, 1936.

ISAACS, SUSAN. Criteria for Interpretation. *Int. J. Psa.*, vol. XX, 1939.

JEKELS, LUDWIG, AND BERGLER, EDMUND. Uebertragung und Liebe. *Imago*, vol. XX, 1934, pp. 5-31.

JELLIFFE, SMITH ELY. Some Notes on Transference. *J. Abnormal Psych.*, vol. VIII, No. 5, 1914, p. 302.

———— *The Technique of Psychoanalysis.* New York: Nervous and Mental Disease Pub. Co., 1914.

———— Contributions to Psychotherapeutic Technique through Psychoanalysis. *Psych. Rev.*, vol. VI, 1919, pp. 1-14.

JOKL, ROBERT HANS. The Mobilizing of the Sense of Guilt. *Int. J. Psa.*, vol. VIII, 1927.

JONES, ERNEST. *Papers on Psychoanalysis.* New York: W. Wood and Co., pp. 731. London: Bailliere, Tindall and Cox, 1913.

———— Bemerkungen zur psychoanalytischen Technik. I. Traeume in der Psychoanalyse. II. Suggestion und Uebertragung. *Int. Ztschr. Psa.*, vol. II, 1914, pp. 274-275.

———— *Treatment of Neuroses.* New York: W. Wood and Co., pp. 233, London: Bailliere, Tindall and Cox, 1920.

———— The Relation of Technique to Theory. *Int. J. Psa.*, vol. VI, 1924, pp. 1-4.

KAISER, HELMUTH. Probleme der Technik. *Int. Ztschr. Psa.*, vol. XX, 1934, pp. 490-522.

KARPMAN, BEN. Psychic Impotence. *Psych. Review*, vol. XX, 1933.

KASANIN, J. Defense Reactions in Anxiety States of Central Origin. *Psych. Quart.*, vol. XI, 1942.

KEMPF, EDWARD J. The Psychoanalytic Treatment of Dementia Praecox. Report of a Case. *Psych. Review*, vol. VI, 1919, pp. 15-58.

KLEIN, MELANIE. *The Psychoanalysis of Children.* London: Hogarth Press, 1932.

Kovacs, Vilma. Beispiele zur aktiven Technik. *Int. Ztschr. Psa.*, vol. XIV, 1928, pp. 405–408.

———— Training-and Control-Analysis. *Int. J. Psa.*, vol. XVII, 1936.

Kubie, Lawrence. *Practical Aspects of Psychoanalysis.* New York: W. W. Norton and Co., 1936.

LaForgue, René. 'Active' Psychoanalytic Technique and the Will to Recovery. *Int. J. Psa.*, vol. X, 1929.

———— Resistances at the Conclusion of Analytic Treatment. *Int. J. Psa.*, vol. XV, 1934.

———— Exceptions to the Fundamental Rule of Psychoanalysis. *Int. J. Psa.*, vol. XVIII, 1937.

Landauer, Karl. 'Passive' Technik. *Int. Ztschr. Psa.*, vol. X, 1924, pp. 415–422.

Lewin, Bertram D. Claustrophobia. *Psych. Quart.*, vol. IV, 1935.

Lewis, Nolan D. C. Additional Observations on the Castration Reaction in Males. *Psych. Review*, vol. XVIII, 1931.

Loewenstein, R. Phallic Passivity in Men. *Int. J. Psa.*, vol. XVI, 1935.

———— Bemerkungen zur Theorie des Therapeutischen Vorganges der Psychoanalyse. *Int. Ztschr. Psa.*, vol. XXIII, 1937, pp. 560–563.

Lorand, Sandor. A Horse Phobia. *Psych. Review*, vol. XIV, 1927.

———— A Narcissistic Neurosis with Hypochondria Symptoms. *Psych. Review*, vol. XV, 1928.

———— Dynamics and Therapy of Depressive States. *Psych. Review*, vol. 24, 1937.

———— Role of the Female Penis Phantasy in Male Character Formation. *Int. J. Psa.*, vol. XX, 1939.

———— *The Morbid Personality.* New York, Alfred A. Knopf, 1931.

Menninger, Karl A. Some Observations on the Psychological Factors in Urination and Genito-Urinary Afflictions. *Psych. Review*, vol. 28, 1941.

Mittelmann, Bela. Euphoric Reactions in the Course of Psychoanalytic Treatment. *Psych. Review*, vol. 27, 1940.

NUNBERG, H. The Will to Recovery. *Int. J. Psa.*, vol. VII, 1926, pp. 64–78.

———— Symposium on the Theory of the Therapeutic Results of Psychoanalysis. *Int. J. Psa.*, vol. XVIII, 1937.

OBERNDORF, C. P. *The Scope and Technique of Psychoanalysis.* Med. Record, 1912.

———— Time—Its Relation to Reality and Purpose. *Psych. Review,* vol. 28, 1941.

PECK, MARTIN W. Negative Transference in Psychoanalysis. *Psych. Review,* vol. XVI, 1929.

PFEIFFER, SIGMUND. On a Form of Defense. *Psych. Quart.,* vol. IX, 1940.

RADO, SANDOR. The Economic Principle in Psychoanalytic Technique. *Int. J. Psa.,* vol. VI, 1925.

———— The Problem of Melancholia. *Int. J. Psa.,* vol. IX, 1928.

———— Developments in the Psychoanalytic Conception and Treatment of Neuroses. *Psych. Quart.,* vol. VIII, 1939.

RANK, OTTO. *The Trauma of Birth and Its Importance for Psychoanalytic Therapy.* New York: Harcourt, Brace and Co., 1924.

REICH, WILHELM. *Der triebhafte Charakter.* Int. Psa. Verlag, 1925.

———— The Sources of Neurotic Anxiety: A Contribution to the Theory of Psychoanalytic Therapy. *Int. J. Psa.,* Vol. VII, 1926, pp. 381–391.

———— Zur Technik der Deutung und der Widerstandsanalyse. *Int. Ztschr. Psa.,* Vol. XIII, 1927, pp. 141–159.

———— Ueber Charakteranalyse. *Int. Ztschr. Psa.,* vol. XIV, 1928, pp. 180–196.

REIK, THEODOR. Some Remarks on the Study of Resistances. *Int. J. Psa.,* vol. V, 1924, pp. 141–154.

———— New Ways in Psychoanalytic Technique. *Int. J. Psa.,* vol. XIV, 1933.

RIVIERE, JOAN. Jealousy as a Mechanism of Defence. *Int. J. Psa.,* vol. XIII, 1932.

———— A Contribution to the Analysis of the Negative Therapeutic Reaction. *Int. J. Psa.,* vol. XVII, 1936.

ROHEIM, GEZA. Psychoanalysis and the Folk-Tale. *Int. J. Psa.,* vol. III, 1922, pp. 180–186.

SACHS, HANNS. Behavior As an Expression of Mental Processes During Analysis. *Int. J. Psa.,* vol. XI, 1930.

SADGER, ISIDOR. Erfolge und Dauer der psychoanalytischen Neurosenbehandlung. *Int. Ztschr. Psa.,* vol. XV, 1929, pp. 426–434.

SAUL, LEON J. Utilization of Early Current Dreams in Formulating Psychoanalytic Cases. *Psych. Quart.,* vol. IX, 1940.

SCHILDER, PAUL. Notes on Psychogenic Depression and Melancholia. *Psych. Review,* vol. XX, 1933.

SCHMIDEBERG, MELITTA. Reassurance As a Means of Analytic Technique. *Int. J. Psa.,* vol. XVI, 1935, pp. 307–324.

———— The Mode of Operation of Psychoanalytic Therapy. *Int. J. Psa.,* vol. XIX, 1938.

———— The Role of Suggestion in Analytic Therapy. *Psych. Review, vol.* 26, 1939.

SEARL, M. N. Some Queries on Principles of Technique. *Int. J. Psa.,* vol. XVII, 1936.

SHARPE, ELLA FREEMAN. The Technique of Psychoanalysis. *Int. J. Psa.,* vol. XI, Part III, 1930.

———— The Technique of Psychoanalysis. *Ibid.* Part IV.

———— The Technique of Psychoanalysis. *Int. J. Psa.,* vol. XII, 1931.

SIMMEL, ERNST. Psychoanalytic Treatment in a Clinic. *Int. J. Psa.,* vol. X, 1929, pp. 70–90.

SLUTSKY, ALBERT. Interpretation of a Resistance: The Analytical Treatment As a Neurotic Defense. *Psych. Quart.,* vol. I, 1932, pp. 345–448.

STEINER, MAXIM. The Dream Symbolism of the Analytical Situation. *Int. J. Psa.,* vol. XVIII, 1937, pp. 294–305.

STERBA, RICHARD. The Fate of the Ego in Analytic Therapy. *Int. J. Psa.,* vol. XV, 1934.

———— The Dynamics of the Dissolution of the Transference Resistance. *Psych. Quart.,* vol. IX, 1940.

———— The Formative Activity of the Analyst. *Int. J. Psa.*, vol. XXV, 1944.

STERN, ADOLPH. On the Counter-Transference in Psychoanalysis. *Psych. Review*, vol. XI, 1924, pp. 166–174.

STRACHEY, JAMES. The Nature of the Therapeutic Action of Psychoanalysis. *Int. J. Psa.*, vol. XV, 1934.

———— Symposium on the Theory of the Therapeutic Results of Psychoanalysis. *Int. J. Psa.*, vol. XVIII, 1937.

TANEYHILL, G. LANE. Notes on Psychoanalytic Technique. *Psych. Review*, vol. III, 1916, p. 461.

THOMPSON, CLARA. Development of Awareness of Transference in a Markedly Detached Personality. *Int. J. Psa.*, vol. XIX, 1938.

WAELDER, ROBERT. The Problem of Freedom in Psychoanalysis and the Problem of Reality Testing. *Int. J. Psa.*, vol. XVII, 1936.

WEISS, EDOARDO. Emotional Memories and Acting Out. *Psych. Quart.*, vol. XI, 1942.

WITTELS, FRITZ. Psychology and Treatment of Depersonalization. *Psych. Review*, vol. 27, 1940.

ZILBOORG, GREGORY. The Fundamental Conflict with Psychoanalysis. *Int. J. Psa.*, vol. XX, 1939, pp. 480–492.

INDEX

Abraham, Karl, 117

"A Child Is Being Beaten", S. Freud, 60

Aggression, 5, 18, 69; towards analyst, 16, 66, 74, 209; of character neurotic, 139, 141, 143, 145, 146, 148, 152; of compulsion neurotic, 120, 121, 124, 126, 129, 131, 134, 135, 205, 206; as defense mechanism, 62; of depressive patient, 179, 183, 184; of female with sex difficulties, 97, 108, 109; of male with sex difficulties, 4, 73, 74, 76, 85; against parents, 43; and rivalry, 41

Alexander, Franz, 123

Ambivalence, 59, 117, 118, 130, 161, 162

Amenorrhea, 158, 170, 175, 177, 198

Anus, anal, 17, 18, 20, 24, 38, 40, 63, 80, 117, 118, 119, 120, 180; tendencies of compulsive neurotic 121; see also sadism, anal

Analysis, active technique in 63, 64; learning method of 1; objective of 155; patient's reaction to 12, 174; phases of 15ff, 20; procedure of 6ff; termination of 223–232

Analyst, X, 1; and attitude towards patient 2f, 5, 9, 23f, 67, 87, 210–222; and active interference 31, 32, 42, 133; and interpretation of patient's attitudes 15–34, 112, 139, 187; see also analysis; dreams, interpretation of; and therapy

Anorexia, 93, 175; nervosa 157, 158, 229

Anxiety, 5, 6, 7, 8, 9, 12, 16, 17, 27, 33, 69, 227; and patients with character difficulties 140, 146, 150, 153; and phobias 35–64, 139; and sex 114, 130, 169

Association, free, 4, 6, 9, 15, 139, 154, 190

Behavior, 9, 11, 12, 15, 16, 203; of character neurotic 139, 140, 144, 145, 148, 149, 152, 153, 154; of depressive neurotic 159, 185; of male with sex difficulties 69; and task of therapy 5, 228, 231, 232

Bisexuality, see sex

Castration, in relation to analysis 48; complex in woman 49, 50, 60, 103, 113, 152, 171; dream of 131; fear of 11, 40, 41, 66, 70, 82, 84, 142; as force towards homosexualism 120; in Oedipus stage 119; threat of 76, 143

Clitoris, 49, 50, 53, 83, 114

Coitus, see sex, intercourse

Complex, inferiority 68, 113, 137; masculinity 230; masculinity—see also castration; masturbation; and penis, masculinity complex

Compulsion, see obsession and neurosis, compulsion